Fruit Kebab à la Troisgros

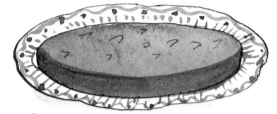

Almond Brown Butter Cake

Martine's Tarte au Citron

Chocolate Soufflé

Crème Chantilly

Orange Honey Mousse

Buckwheat Crêpes

Tisane

Fanny in France

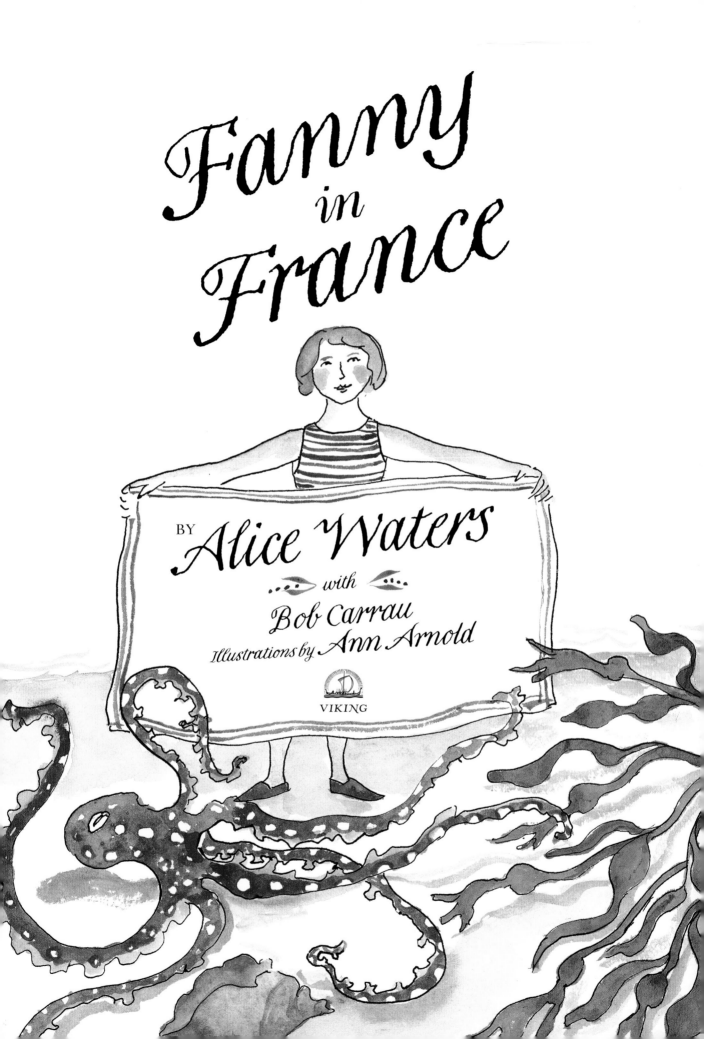

Fanny in France

BY Alice Waters

with

Bob Carrau

Illustrations by Ann Arnold

VIKING

À ma famille française

VIKING

Penguin Young Readers Group

An imprint of Penguin Random House LLC

375 Hudson Street

New York, New York 10014

First published in the United States of America by Viking, an imprint of Penguin Random House LLC, 2016

LIBRARY OF CONGRESS CATALOGING-IN-PUBLICATION DATA

Names: Waters, Alice, author. | Carrau, Bob, author. | Arnold, Ann, date– illustrator.

Title: Fanny in France : Travel Adventures of a Chef's Daughter, with Recipes by Alice Waters with Bob Carrau ; illustrated by Ann Arnold.

Description: New York : VIKING, published by Penguin Group, [2016] | Audience: Ages 10+. | Audience: Grades 7 to 8.

Identifiers: LCCN 2016011994 | ISBN 9780670016662 (hardcover)

Subjects: LCSH: Singer, Fanny, date—Travel—France—Juvenile literature. | Chez Panisse—Juvenile literature. | Cooking, French—Juvenile literature.

Classification: LCC TX652.5 .W3594 2016 | DDC 641.5944—dc23 LC record available at http://lccn.loc.gov/2016011994.

Manufactured in China

1 3 5 7 9 10 8 6 4 2

Contents

Fanny's French Adventures 7

Fanny's French Recipes 89

    Le Pain 92

        Flatbread 94

        Baguettes 95

        Croûtons 96

        Bread Crumbs 97

    Hors d'Oeuvres 98

        François's Marinated Olives 99

        Slow-Roasted Almonds with Sage Leaves 100

        Oeuf Mayonnaise 101

        Crudités 103

        Vinaigrette 105

        Gougères (Cheese Puffs) 106

        Tapenade 108

    Les Potages 110

        Potage de Cresson (Watercress Soup) 111

        Soupe au Pistou 112

        Chicken Broth 115

        Soupe à l'Ail (Garlic Soup) 117

    Petits Repas 118

        Omelet 119

        Croque-Monsieur (Grilled Cheese Sandwich) 120

Salade Niçoise (Salad from Nice) 121

Pizza with Quick Tomato Sauce 123

Plats Principaux 126

Martine's Roast Chicken with Smoked Paprika and Mustard . 127

Tomatoes à la Provençale 129

Beans Cooked over the Fire 130

Bouillabaisse (Provençal Fish Soup) 132

Couscous Royal with Chermoula 137

Steak Frites 141

Pommes Frites (Crispy Pan-Fried Potatoes) 143

Fish en Papillote (Fish in Parchment Paper Packages) 145

Roasted Herbed Rack of Lamb 148

Potatoes au Gratin 149

Les Salades 152

Mesclun Salad 153

Baked Goat Cheese with Garden Lettuces 154

Les Desserts 156

Buckwheat Crêpes 157

Orange Honey Mousse 158

Chocolate Soufflé 160

Crème Chantilly 162

Fruit Kebab à la Troisgros 162

Martine's Tarte au Citron (Lemon Tart) 164

Almond Brown Butter Cake 167

Tisanes (Herbal Infusions) 169

Les Confitures 170

Plum Jam 171

Roasted Strawberry Jam 172

Translation of French Words and Phrases 174

Fanny's French Adventures

Bonjour. Je m'appelle Fanny et j'ai neuf ans. That means, "Hi. I'm Fanny and I'm nine years old," in French. I know how to speak French because, even though I live in California, I go to a school where everyone speaks French most of the day. At first it was horrible! On the first day of school I didn't know any French words, and all the teachers talked to us *only* in French!

"Bienvenue, les enfants! Avez-vous passé un bon été?"

I didn't know what they were saying or what they wanted us to do! It was like being on another planet.

"S'il vous plaît, asseyez-vous! Ouvrez vos cahiers et prenez vos crayons!"

Some of the kids could already speak French, so they knew what was going on—but not me. Even if we just wanted a little graham cracker at snack time we had to ask for it in French or we wouldn't get one. I had to ask my friends how to say *"S'il vous plaît, madame, est-ce que je peux avoir un biscuit?"* Or I just went hungry. Which is funny, because I grew up at a restaurant and I know lots of things about cooking and food.

Luckily, every day my mom packed me a really good lunch. There were always special things like little containers filled with salad leaves, with pansy and marigold petals mixed in. And a separate container for the *vinaigrette* so the salad wouldn't get soggy. Sometimes there were strawberries sliced in orange juice. And, of course, garlic toast! The other kids—and even some of the teachers—couldn't help but notice. We started sharing and trading things from each other's lunch boxes. It was really fun. And that was how I started to learn French—by asking other kids around the table what was in their lunch boxes and giving them a little bite of what was in mine.

Now I can speak French better than either of my parents! And I can talk to all the cooks at Chez Panisse who come from France to cook. Sometimes I even help my mom find the perfect French word for a menu she's writing.

Chez Panisse is the name of the restaurant run by my mom and a bunch of her friends. It feels like another home to me. Maybe that's because before it became a restaurant, it actually *was* a house! Lots of times I go there after school to play or try to help out or just wait for my mom to take me home. There's a huge poster on the upstairs café wall that has a big picture of a pretty girl on it and my name. When people ask me about it, I tell them, "That's the original Fanny—the one my mom named me after."

It's true! That poster is from an old French movie that my mom loves. The movie is called *Fanny* and it's about a girl much older than me who lived in France almost a hundred years ago. The French Fanny lived in a city by the sea that's still there, called Marseille. She sold fish down by the harbor and fell in love with her handsome next-door neighbor, whose name was Marius. But Marius went on a long voyage and was gone for so long that Fanny thought he would never return. So, after crying a lot, Fanny decided to marry another man who also loved her. That man, who had a store that sold sails for ships and sailboats, was named Panisse. So my mom named her restaurant Chez Panisse to remind her of the man who loved and took care of Fanny.

My mom loves old French movies—especially if they're in black and white. And especially if they're made by Marcel Pagnol, a famous French film director. I always want to watch something else, but my mom is always saying, "Oh, Fanny, let's watch *Harvest*!" Or, "We haven't seen *César* in a while." I think I'm the only kid in Berkeley who's seen *The Baker's Wife* more times than *The Little Mermaid*.

She always laughs and cries when she watches these movies. I don't really know why. But, no matter what, after she's done, she starts cooking. She puts on some French music and asks me to help her peel

garlic or pick some lettuce out back in the garden. Sometimes she gets on the phone and calls one of her friends in France, like Martine or Lulu, because those movies have reminded her of them so much. And, if we're really lucky, my mom starts to plan a trip.

I'm always so happy when she does this, because I know my dad and I get to go with her. We've been to France lots of times—even when I was a baby—and every time we go, I have great adventures and see lots of friends and make lots of new ones.

Sometimes when we go, I pretend we're going on an old sailing ship, just like the one Marius sailed away on when he left Fanny in the harbor of Marseille. I pack my suitcase like it's a big trunk, and when we're on the plane, I pretend it's a big floating boat traveling through the sky. And all I think about is who we're going to see when we get there, what we're going to do, and where we're going to go. I pretend all our friends will be waiting at a dock, cheering, *"Bienvenue!"*

$\mathcal{E}$very time we go to France, we visit Lulu and Lucien. Lulu and Lucien live in a big old house near Marseille that's right in the middle of the vineyards. We call their house the *Domaine,* and there are pine trees all around it that look like huge umbrellas. You can almost see the Mediterranean Sea from their front garden.

My mom says Lulu and Lucien—whose last name is Peyraud—are like her French parents, so I guess that means they're like my French grandparents. Lulu and I always give each other presents when we first see each other. One time, Lulu gave me an old necklace with a painted bird on it. I always give her drawings I made in school. And then we give each other a big hug. I love hugging Lulu, because she's almost my size. Lucien pours drinks—a glass of rosé for my mom and dad and, for me, some sparkling water with a little wine in it. And there's always a little something Lulu's made to eat, like *tapenade* on toast.

Lulu and Lucien have a big family, and most of them live nearby. Their oldest son, Jean-Marie, comes out of the wine cellar where he's been making wine all day to say hello. And Catherine, his wife, pops out of the office where she's been working. Their other son, François, and his wife, Paule, hear we're around and come down from their house on the other side of the vineyards—usually bringing figs they've picked or olives that François has made with wild fennel. Their daughter Véronique, comes up from her café in Bandol and brings her daughter Manon, who is exactly my age and my absolute best friend in France. And, if we're lucky, their other daughter, Laurence, will be visiting from Paris, and some of Lulu and Lucien's other grandkids, too—like Valérie and Jérôme. There are a lot of Peyrauds! It's just like the sign on the driveway says: *Attention! Un Peyraud peut en cacher un autre!* which means "Careful! One Peyraud may be hiding behind another!"

14

When everyone's together, Lucien toasts to *"notre famille américaine,"* which means "our American family." And everybody clinks glasses.

Then, after a while, Lulu takes my hand and leads me into the house. We climb up the winding stairs to my special bedroom on the top floor. This room always feels like magic to me because the ceiling is so low. Anyone who's not a kid has to hunch over to walk around inside it. There are little beds just my size and a million places to crawl into and hide. I always think hobbits live there when I'm not around.

I always have good dreams when I stay at Lulu and Lucien's house.

$\mathcal{L}$ulu loves fish. I think it's because she swims every day in the Bay of Bandol. She must see them out there when she's swimming and then get hungry for them.

You have to get up really early if you're going to the fish market with Lulu. She likes to be the first one there, because that's when she can find the fish that were just caught and that come from nearby. Lulu knows all the fish sellers by name and says *"Bonjour"* and *"Ça va?"* to them. She looks at what's on everyone's tables and sees if any fish catch her eye. The eyes of the fish tell Lulu if they're good or not—if the fish's eyes are shiny and clear and they look right back at her, then she knows it's good to eat.

Lulu likes the little red fish best—they're called *rougets*. I found some pretty ones once and tried to point them out to her, but when I turned around, Lulu was gone!

"I know where you can find Lulu," one of the fish sellers said. And she pointed toward the water.

And, sure enough, there she was—down on the dock, buying some *rougets* from a fisherman right off his boat. I guess that way Lulu knew for sure that those fish were the most alive.

$\mathcal{I}$ still remember the first time I was at the Domaine when they made *bouillabaisse*. I could tell right away when I woke up that something special was going on. The fire that François had started outside smelled so good. He'd used dried grape vines as wood, so the air everywhere smelled just like grapes.

Lulu had invited the whole family and some friends over, and everybody was going to help cook. It took all day. Lulu cut up the pretty fish she'd bought at the market and put all the bones into a big copper pot. Then she hung the pot over the fire. Jean-Marie found some white wine to put in the pot, and Manon and I picked herbs from the garden. We gave the herbs to Lulu, and she sprinkled them in the pot. I got to put in the saffron—my favorite thing! You have to put in just the tiniest bit. Lulu stirred it all around and sniffed it to make sure it smelled just right. I could tell it did when she kissed her fingers.

Then we helped Paule peel garlic. She smashed it in the mortar for a *rouille*. After that, we helped Catherine cut up plums for a tart. My friend Tonio's dad, Kermit, always wants to open a bottle of wine, so Jean-Marie and Lucien went to the cellar and came up with some rosé. My dad is always hungry, so he grilled some bread, and Valérie rubbed garlic and olive oil on it, and we all had a little snack. I asked Lulu if she wanted some of my water because she'd been working so hard in the

kitchen, and she said, "No thanks, *ma petite chérie*—I only drink wine. If I drink water, I'll rust!" I think she's kidding when she says this—but maybe not?

Tonio's mom, Gail, and Jérôme washed the salad that my mom picked. Jérôme did most of the work, because Gail couldn't stop taking pictures with her camera—even of the cat!

"Now it's time to put the fish in," Lulu said, and she dropped them one by one into the bubbling soup. Paule dipped a big spoon into the pot to taste. She licked her lips because it was tasting good.

Tonio and his sister, Marley, helped Laurence set the big table. They had to use three tablecloths to cover the whole thing, and stacks and stacks of plates and tons of silverware. I asked, "Why so many places?" and Lucien told me, "It's the end of the grape harvest, Fanny. All the workers who helped take care of the vines are coming to celebrate together. It's an old tradition."

He was right, because soon after that, even more people started to arrive, and that was good because the *bouillabaisse* was almost done.

When no one was looking, Manon and I snuck up the stairs to my magic bedroom. We opened a huge trunk that's filled with old clothes and costumes and we tried lots of things on and dressed up just like gypsies. We came down and everyone asked, "Where are *Manon et Fanny*?" We shrugged and said we didn't know. But we asked if we could eat some *bouillabaisse* anyway.

Laurence asked "the gypsies" to get some flowers for the table. We went into the garden and decided to pick only flowers you could eat. So we picked pea-plant flowers and basil-plant flowers and some

blue borage flowers and some yellow mustard flowers and even some purple chive flowers. We put them all together and my mom said, "*Regardez!* Edible bouquets!"

"*Magnifique!*" Lucien said. We put the bouquets on the table and told Lucien he could only look at them and smell them. He had to wait until *after* dinner if he wanted to eat them with the salad.

"I don't know if I can wait," he replied, laughing.

Everyone sat down at the table. Lulu and François spooned the *bouillabaisse* into big bowls. Manon and I put a grilled *croûton* spread with *rouille* in each one and helped pass them around. Jean-Marie opened a special wine that had been made right there. He tipped the wine carefully into each glass so everyone could have a taste—he even poured a little for me. Lucien made a toast thanking everyone for making the harvest a good one. We all said, *"Santé!"* and then Lulu took her seat and everyone started to eat. The *bouillabaisse* was so good!

After dinner everyone was happy and full. And when the sun went down, a *vendangeur* pulled out an accordion, and pretty soon everyone was singing and dancing to the music.

When François goes swimming, he snorkels around and brings up lots of different things to eat. One time, he pulled up a huge octopus. It was scary. He got it from under a rock. It was all brown and slippery and inky. He said we should eat it, so we took it back to Lulu and Lucien's house and made a kind of octopus stew. I had the hardest job—washing the octopus. Every time I tried to scrub it, the tentacle suckers sucked onto my hand. Yuck! The stew didn't look so good—it was all black and slimy—but it tasted delicious. And luckily those tentacles didn't suck onto the insides of anyone's mouth as we ate.

Another time, François came out of the water holding a spiny purple sea urchin. It was so weird—it looked like a sea porcupine.

He cut a hole in the sea urchin's shell with his knife and offered everyone bites of the creamy orange insides—right there on the beach. Tonio loves sea urchins. He took a bite right away, but I gagged and backed off. "Don't worry, Fanny," Tonio said. "Just try it. It tastes sort of sweet, like peaches with a little salt." I didn't believe him, but I finally took a really little bite. And you know what? Tonio was right.

I always knew I was named after a girl from an old French movie, but I didn't really know how special my name was until I went bike-riding around the island of Bendor with Manon. Bendor is in the middle of the Bay of Bandol. You

can only get there by boat, and they never let cars on it at all!
Bendor has lots of beaches and little hotels and cafés all over it,
and everyone goes there to go swimming and walking or to have
picnics and just have fun.

Manon and I found two bikes in the cellar of the Domaine. The bikes were so dusty and rusty, they looked like they hadn't been ridden in years. *"Pas de problème!"* Manon said. But of course she gave me the rustier bike.

Everyone came down to the pier to see us off. I had never been anywhere without adults before, but my mom said, "If you stick together and are back in two hours, you can go." Manon and I proudly rolled our bikes onto the ferryboat and waved good-bye. The captain blew the boat whistle, and off we went! And then, after three minutes, we were there, because Bendor isn't really that far.

Manon and I set off right away. We rode our bikes up and down and all over everywhere. We saw swimmers and walkers and fishermen and kids out playing soccer and people taking in the sights. *Tout le monde* was out having fun. Including us. That is, until I heard a scary hissing sound. I looked down and saw I had a flat tire. *"Mon dieu!"* I cried. "What are we going to do?"

"Pas de problème!" Manon said. "We'll just go to that café over there and ask for help."

We rolled our bikes—mine going *bumpety-bump*—up to the café. It was totally filled with people having lunch and *apéritifs*. We tried to get the owner's attention, but he was so busy running around waiting on tables and seating people, he didn't even see us.

A lady eating a *pan bagnat* asked us what was wrong. We showed her the tire. She said, "You poor girls . . . what are your names?"

"*Manon et Fanny,*" we said.

"*Manon et Fanny!*" the lady exclaimed. "*C'est pas possible!* Just like in the movies! *Vous êtes les filles de Pagnol! Tout le monde! C'est Manon et Fanny!*"

The whole restaurant turned and looked at us. You see, Manon got her name from *Manon des Sources,* which is another one of those old black-and-white French movies that my mom really likes. The café owner dropped everything and rushed over to help us. We showed him the tire. He immediately took us around back to where his son, one of the waiters, had a little tool bench. The son fixed my tire in no time. He was good.

The café owner was so proud to have *Manon et Fanny* at his restaurant that he gave us our own special table right up front. And then he brought us fancy *citrons pressés*. We were having so much fun, we totally forgot what time it was. Until we heard the ferryboat whistle! Then we jumped up and said, *"Merci!"* and grabbed our bikes and dashed toward the ferry.

My mom says Lulu used to swim to the island of Bendor all by herself when she was a young girl—can you believe it? She would put all her clothes in a little waterproof knapsack and strap it on her back and swim between the boats. When she got to Bendor, she'd come out of the water and secretly change into her dry clothes and then go meet her boyfriend, Lucien, for a secret rendezvous. *Incroyable!*

One time Lulu said, "Let's go walk *le Circuit Pagnol*." The Pagnol Circuit—which is how you say it in English—is a hike through the countryside where lots of Pagnol's movies were made. Lulu, my mom, my dad, and I all made a picnic, and we got into Lulu's car and drove up into the hills above Marseille. My dad was driving and Lulu was yelling out directions to him on the curvy mountain roads—*"À droite! À gauche! À droite!"* I laughed so hard watching my dad trying to keep up with Lulu's directions—"Right! Left! Right!" Lulu said her directions were *"Comme la politique!"* which I guess is a funny joke, but I didn't totally get it.

In the mountains, we hiked up a steep, rocky trail. It was so hard. Finally we came to a pretty village, but no one lived there anymore.

"Why doesn't anyone live here?" I asked.

"Over the years the young people couldn't make money in these villages anymore," Lulu said. "So they left for jobs in the big cities like Marseille or Nice or Lyon or Paris."

"Why couldn't they make money here?" I asked.

"Because farming and living off the land is hard," my mom said.

"And the young people thought they could make money more easily in the city," my dad added.

"Ah ... la vie," Lulu said. "This village reminds me of Jean Giono—one of my favorite French writers. He lived close-by and wrote some of the stories that Marcel Pagnol turned into those movies your mom loves, Fanny."

I knew who Jean Giono was because my mom always reads me a book he wrote called *The Man Who Planted Trees*. That book is about a shepherd who lived up in the mountains. But the mountains were totally bare, because the people who used to live there had cut all the trees down so they could build houses and make charcoal for their fires. It was so bare that, when it rained, nothing would catch the rainfall. And so everybody just moved away. But this shepherd stayed. And as he walked through the mountains with his sheep, he would plant acorns everywhere. So after many years, lots of trees grew. And the mountains weren't bare anymore. The trees could catch the rain, so the streams started running again. And because the streams were running again, birds and animals came back to live in the forests. And then the people who used to live in the villages saw how beautiful it was and came back too.

We decided to have our lunch right in the middle of that village and pretend we lived there for a while. We spread our picnic out on the grass and made sandwiches and shared cheese and fruit. We lay in the sun and we all tried to imagine what life was like in that village many years ago. Before we left, I took a peach pit from a peach I was eating and I planted it in the ground. I thought maybe someday it would grow and there'd be a peach tree in that village. And someone else might come by and see it and eat a peach from it. And who knows? Maybe they'd decide to stay. . . .

It's always fun to go to Richard's house. He's a friend of Lulu's and my mom's, and he lives way up a winding mountain road. When you get there, you can see his art studio and jump into his swimming pool that is cut right into a rock.

One time, Lulu and my mom and I went for lunch, but none of us saw any food anywhere. Richard's kitchen was totally empty. And we were all starving!

Richard asked me if I'd help him make lunch. I said, *"Bien sûr,"* but I was thinking, "With *what*?" Richard saw what I was thinking and laughed. He said, "Don't worry, Fanny, everything we need to make a delicious *salade niçoise* is right outside these doors."

The first thing we did was go down to Richard's chicken coop. At the chicken coop, Richard introduced me to some really nice chickens who let us take some of the eggs they'd just laid.

Next, we stepped into Richard's kitchen garden. We picked lots of different kinds of greens.

Richard said this was *mesclun* salad and these plants were really special. They grew only around the place where he lived. We also picked green beans and tomatoes and a huge head of garlic that was hard to pull out of the ground! Richard said we had most of the ingredients we needed for lunch. That's when I realized the reason Richard doesn't keep very much food in his kitchen is that most of the things he cooks with are living right outside his house.

It turned out Richard did have *some* food in his kitchen—like olives in a jar and anchovies in salt—

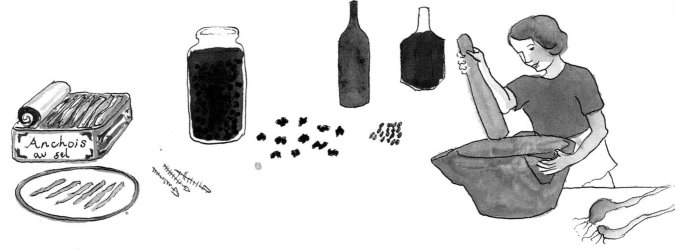

but these were hidden away. So we boiled the eggs, topped and tailed the beans, washed the lettuces, cut the tomatoes, pitted the olives, cleaned the anchovies—yuck!—and mashed the garlic in a huge mortar. We used some of Richard's very special homemade vinegar to make the *vinaigrette.* It was so much fun, and the salad tasted especially great.

And, of course, Richard had a *baguette* to go with it.

"It isn't so much what your nose looks like," Kermit says. "It's what it can smell!"

Kermit loves wine. His favorite thing to do is taste wine before it's even in bottles. We went with him once to visit his friend Gérard, who makes wine right next to his house. Gérard was really nice, but I think he was wondering what a kid was doing on a wine-tasting trip. "Don't worry, Gérard," Kermit said. "Fanny has a great nose. She will impress you. You will see." I'm not sure Gérard believed him, but he took us into his wine cellar anyway.

We followed Gérard underground down a dark dirt ramp. The lower we got, the colder it was. I was glad my mom had told me to bring my jacket.

At the bottom of the ramp was a huge, dark room with lots of wine bottles stacked in big towers. Some of the bottles looked like they'd been there for hundreds of years! It was kind of scary, because it looked like there were spider webs hanging everywhere.

"Those aren't spider webs," Kermit said. "That's just mold. It's good for the wine. It catches the water and keeps the corks moist and plump while the wine is aging."

"We have an old saying in France," Gérard said. "If you build a cellar and the mold doesn't come, you need to build another cellar!"

"I guess this is a good cellar!" I said.

We all laughed. Then Gérard took some white wine out of a huge wooden barrel and poured each of us a glass. He told us this was his newest wine—he was just making it. Gérard swirled his wine around in his glass. Then he dropped his long nose into it and took a deep sniff. Then Kermit did the same thing. Then my dad and mom did the same thing. So I thought, *I'd better do it too.*

"Well, what do you think, Fanny?" Kermit asked.

"It smells like apricots," I said, because it did.

"*Oui,*" Gérard said. "*Moi aussi!*" Which meant he thought so too. I think he started to like me then. . . .

Gérard got some red wine out of another huge barrel and we all smelled that. I thought this one smelled like wild strawberries, but then I wasn't so sure because it also smelled like red cherries. Gérard smiled when he heard this. He said that when wines are fermenting, they have a life of their own and they are always changing—every day. He said my nose must be very special to have smelled that!

"Fanny has a special nose for lots of things," my dad said. "Like getting into trouble."

Whatever you do, don't get lost in the market in Nice. I did once and I'll never forget it. The market in Nice is really crowded and goes up and down all these steps and winds through all these streets and just goes all over the place. It's huge. There are so many people selling so many things that you can get really turned around. That's how I lost my mom. One minute she was buying cinnamon and vanilla beans, and the next minute she was gone. I yelled, "Mama! Mama!" but none of the hundreds of people paid any attention. I started to get really scared and looked everywhere for her. She wasn't near the fruit stands, she wasn't near the bean sellers, she wasn't near the sandal places, she wasn't under the garlic strands, she wasn't by the olive barrels, she wasn't near the spice sellers, she wasn't by the pepper people or the eggplant vendors or the *socca* sellers. I got so worried, I even went into a coffee store and a tobacco shop—yuck! I was starting to wonder if I was ever going to see my mom again or if I was going to have to live the rest of my life with the stray cats in the market.

Then, suddenly, outside a little delicatessen, I smelled something very familiar and sweet. I looked over and saw a lady sitting and eating one of the chickpea fritters they call *panisses*. On her table was a bunch of tango roses—my mom's favorite flower. My mom says tango roses smell so good, they use them in her favorite perfumes. I went up to the lady and said in my best French, *"Excusez-moi, madame, c'est une jolie fleur. Où l'avez-vouz achetée?"* The woman pointed down the street to a big flower stand. *"Merci,"* I said and ran down to it.

The flower stand had lots of pretty flowers I like, like violets and lavender, but there were also some of the most beautiful tango roses I'd ever seen. And guess what? Standing right in the middle of them was my mom.

$\mathcal{Y}$ou can never lose our friend Nathalie in the market because she dresses in such bright, colorful clothes. Sometimes she looks just like a wild gypsy. She wears silver bracelets and necklaces dangling from everywhere. And sometimes Nathalie even hennas her hair the color of fire, so you can never miss that!

The first time I went with Nathalie to the market in Bonnieux, where she lives, I didn't have a basket. She said, "Fanny, you can't go to the market without a basket. If you don't take a basket, you'll end up using plastic bags. And we can't have that!" So Nathalie gave me a little straw basket that was just the right size for me. It had leather handles on it. I loved it!

Nathalie knows everyone at the market and makes sure she stops at everybody's table to say hello. She asks Monsieur Philippe, the herb seller, how his wife is. She asks the chicken and egg sellers, Madame and Monsieur Toussaint, how their daughter's wedding was. They all ask Nathalie about her sons, Jérôme and Alexandre—they both live in the United States. But even as she's talking, Nathalie is looking carefully over everything. She always likes to buy from her friends,

but she won't buy anything unless it's perfectly ripe. Nathalie's very picky. She looks at about twenty goat cheeses before she chooses just the right one.

Nathalie has me taste things too, like tiny red *fraises des bois*, which are wild strawberries that grow in the woods. They are my favorite things in the world. I even got my mom to plant some in our backyard in Berkeley. She planted one plant here and one plant there, so that finding the ripe berries in our garden feels like hunting for them in the woods.

Nathalie asked me to pick out the carrots for lunch. She said I couldn't put any carrots in my basket unless I'd tasted them and liked them. This was a huge job, because there were a million different kinds of carrots at that market! I had to look at and taste every kind! I said over and over again in my best French, *"Est-ce que je peux goûter les carottes?"* I ate so many carrots that day that when we got home, I didn't even want lunch. But then I smelled the baked goat cheese with bread crumbs that Nathalie was cooking, and I just had to have a few little bites. . . .

My mom's friend Martine is an artist. She and her husband, Claude, live in the hills above Nice. They call their house *La Villa les Clairs Matins*, and it's just like a big magical treasure chest. All the rooms are filled with old and beautiful things that Martine has made or found. There are lots of paintings and photographs and pretty furniture and, my favorite, printed wallpaper. There are also a billion quilts and pillows everywhere that you can make the best beds and forts out of. But you have to be really careful at Villa les Clairs Matins, because everything is held together with just little pieces of string or tape and it's really easy to knock things over and break them. *"Tant pis!"* Martine says when this happens. "When you use things, they break. It's sad, but it's better to use beautiful things every day than to put them away in closets and cupboards where no one sees them."

Martine loves special days and *fêtes* because then she gets to set a really special table. One time I went to a flea market with her to look for treasures for my mom's birthday dinner. "We don't have much money, Fanny, but we can still make the table beautiful!"

We searched high and low through all the old paintings and furniture and silverware and glasses. "It's amazing, isn't it, Fanny?" Martine said. "All the things people used so many years ago, we can now use again." Martine picked up a wooden candlestick and said, *"Regarde, Fanny, très spécial, non?"* It just looked normal to me, but Martine showed me that on its side there was a little painting of a rose.

It even looked like a tango rose! Then I could see why the candlestick was so special.

We also found a huge tablecloth stuck behind a mirror. It had even more beautiful roses embroidered on it. *"Ah! Très belle, n'est-ce pas?"* Martine said. She offered the seller half the price that he wanted. He got kind of mad. But Martine talked to him, and I thought they were going to get into a fight, but they smiled at each other and agreed on a price they both liked. The seller even gave me a piece of candy after he wrapped the tablecloth up in paper and string.

Then Martine spotted a set of old dessert plates with pictures of different fruits on each one. I saw that a couple of them had chips on them and showed her. "Ah . . . What's a little chip?" Martine said. "They're still *magnifique*! You're still pretty even when you have a scrape on your knee!"

I found something really special after that. Buried under a stuffed bear was a huge linen napkin with the initial *F* sewed into it. *"Ah! Parfait!"* Martine exclaimed. She dug deeper and found even more napkins. We picked one for each person coming to the party—each with his or her own initial on it!

When we got home, we made my mom stay in the other room while we set the table. Once the candles were lit and the food was ready, Martine said, *"À table!"* My mom came in and the whole dining room glittered. I think my mom cried, she was so happy.

P.S. Never go swimming in the ocean with Claude. He thinks it's funny to pretend there are sea monsters lurking around the rocks. One time he made noises like a sea monster and put kelp on his head like a crazy wig, and it scared not only me but all the other kids on the beach, so everyone ran away!

45

Martine says you should only buy enough food for the day you're going to use it, and you should never buy more food than you can put in your basket or carry home. My mom learned this lesson the hard way one time when she went to the market to buy salad for Martine.

My mom's favorite salad is *mesclun*—the same kind of salad Richard has in his garden. *Mesclun* means "a mix of things." I always think *mesclun* looks a little like lawn cuttings, but it's really the small plants that farmers weed away from the bigger plants so the bigger ones have space to grow. My mom found her favorite *mesclun* seller, and the salad looked so good to her that day that she bought everything he had. My mom bought so much salad that the farmer had to give it all to her wrapped in the big dish towel that he'd used to bring it to the market that morning. This way my mom could actually carry it home by herself. My mom looked like she had a huge salad pillow on her back as she walked through town!

When she got back to Martine's house, she was so proud. But Martine said, "What is this? Who's going to eat all that?"

"But it's so beautiful," my mom said. "Surely it will all get eaten up." Martine told my mom if there was any salad left after dinner, she was never going to let her buy salad again.

Well, that night, to make sure there was no salad left after dinner, my mom ate so much, she looked like a rabbit sitting at the table. "It's a wonder I still even like *mesclun* after that," she says.

Another day, we helped Martine cook a dinner for eight friends. First we went to the butcher, and Martine asked for a nice chicken. My mom couldn't believe it.

"One chicken, Martine?" my mom said. "For nine people? You can't cook just one chicken for nine people! There won't be enough!"

Martine told my mom it was plenty. They got into a big, funny argument in front of the butcher. Martine kept telling my mom over and over again that it was wasteful to buy too much food. And *très cher*!

"But people will go home hungry!" my mom said.

"No, they won't!" Martine told her. "Trust me. One chicken is *tout ce qu'il faut!*"

That afternoon at Martine's house, we helped her cook. First, we went out into her backyard and picked a basketful of herbs and lettuce and vegetables. We made *sauce verte* with the herbs and grilled fennel and sliced eggplant for a *gratin*. Martine asked me to draw a menu for the dinner. Here's the menu I drew:

Dinner for Friends
at Villa les Clairs Matins
Oeufs Farcis with Chicken Liver Toast
Grilled Fennel with Olive Oil and Lemon
Roasted Chicken
with Tapenade and Eggplant Gratin
Mesclun Salad
Martine's Nectarine Galette

Martine was right—one chicken was more than enough! Because we'd made so many other little things to go with it, we didn't need as much of the chicken as my mom thought. Martine even used the leftover chicken bones the next day to make my mom and me a delicious soup for lunch.

The *mistral* is a scary wind that comes out of nowhere and blows for days. It's a wind that dries everything out and drives everyone crazy. Branches fly off trees. Other trees fall over and crash to the ground. Grape vines get their leaves ripped off and fruit trees lose their blossoms. All the fishermen have to tie their boats down in the harbor or they'll float away and crash. Even the cows and horses and chickens and dogs and cats run for cover. Everybody hides in their houses. And even though it's hot, you're supposed to keep all your doors and windows closed to keep the wind out.

We didn't know this during one bad *mistral*, and we kept the front door of Kermit and Gail's house wide open. We were eating lunch, and suddenly we heard a strange buzzing sound. At first we didn't know what it was, but then Tonio saw lots of wasps hovering inside the front door! The wasps were lost and scared and confused because of the wind. And they were mad and crazy and just trying to find a place to hide inside the house! More and more were coming in every second. We didn't know what to do!

But then Marley got an idea. She remembered that wasps go away when there's smoke. So she lit a couple of rosemary branches on

fire and went under the wasps and waved the branches like sticks of incense. It kind of worked, but because the wind was so strong, more wasps kept coming in and Marley had to run away. "It's a good idea," my mom said. "You just don't have enough rosemary!" So she went outside and cut a whole lot of rosemary branches—almost a whole bush—and lit them all on fire. She rolled the whole thing under the wasps like a smoking tumbleweed. Sure enough, the wasps flew, one by one, out the door, and we shut it! Phew!

When we got up the next day, the *mistral* had died down and we could open up all the windows. Everything was back to normal, but Kermit and Gail's house smelled like rosemary for days. And every time I went outside, I kept an eye out for those wasps.

P.S. Richard always says that during a *mistral* all he wants to do is stick his head under a pillow. Now I know what he means!

*C*orsica is an island in the middle of the Mediterranean Sea. Its mountains are *très sauvages*. They have really tall jagged peaks with wild rivers and tumbling waterfalls everywhere. The forests are filled with huge old chestnut trees that drop their spiky shells when it gets windy. You have to be really careful walking then! All the towns have gray stone buildings, and when you wake up in the mornings you always hear bells—sometimes it's church bells and other times it's little bells on goats and sheep. Sometimes you even hear gunshots, because there are lots of hunters out in the woods looking for wild boar.

One time my mom and I went to Corsica with a bunch of friends from California, and we stayed in an old stone house that had a stone bread oven right outside the kitchen door. We didn't think the oven worked at first, because it was so dirty and covered with spider webs and branches and filled with rusty tools and bags. But Tony said, "I bet we can get this thing going." He and Sue and I spent almost a whole day cleaning it out and stacking wood. It was hard work. But when it was clean, we lit a big fire and, sure enough, the whole thing heated up and got hot enough to cook in.

We started making bread in it right away. First, we made some crackers because they're kind of easy. Then we made some pizzas. And those were good.

There was a vegetable truck that would come through town every day. It would honk its funny horn and my mom and I would run down

to see what we could get to cook. We started cooking lots of things in that oven besides bread: we cooked fish and beans and potatoes and eggs. Bob tried to make some flatbread with chestnut flour and it was a disaster! And then when David got there from Paris, he showed us all how to grow our own yeast so we could make real bread that rose.

Our friend Sylviane, who lived nearby and grew up in the old house, was so excited when she saw the bread oven working. She told us that there were eleven other ovens like it all over the town. She said that, in the old days, whenever anybody got a fire going in one, all the neighbors who lived near that oven would come and bake bread in it. That way no one wasted wood.

Sylviane also said each family had their own stamp and stamped their bread with it so when the baking was done, everyone could tell which bread was theirs. I decided to make a stamp for our bread. I drew a picture of a wild boar getting hit on the head by a falling chestnut. Tony helped me make a stamp out of it with wire. Here's what it looked like:

I think our bread tasted way better with that stamp on it!

Our friend Mark liked making bread in that oven so much that when he went home to Bolinas, California, he built his own bread oven in his backyard and started baking bread for all his friends. I wonder what his stamp looks like.

P.S. Someone said Napoleon's mother was born in the house we stayed in. I'm not sure. But I do know Napoleon was born in Corsica and he has the same birthday as *moi*! You know who else has the same birthday as me? That famous chef Julia Child. *Mais oui!*

$\mathcal{I}$ love pizza so much, but my mom says it's hard to find a place that makes real pizza anymore. One time, near the beach in Bordeaux, my mom saw a pizza restaurant with a wood-burning oven. "We can try that place," she said.

We went in and looked around and noticed that the pizzas on everyone's plates didn't look very good. My mom wanted to leave, but I said, "Please! I love pizza!"

"Okay, I have an idea," my mom said. "Let's order the simplest pizzas they have—the ones with no toppings. Just some cheese."

So we did that, and while I waited for the pizzas to be cooked, my mom raced next door to a market. She found some tomatoes and basil and olives. She raced back to the pizza restaurant just as our pizzas were done. At our table, we made our own pizza toppings with the things my mom had gotten. We tore and scattered the basil leaves and we cut up the tomatoes into tiny bits. Then we put the olives all around. Those pizzas were delish!

I think the pizzas were so good that the pizza maker started buying all his toppings from the market next door.

$\mathcal{A}$nother time, it was the hottest day in Bordeaux ever. There were fires all over the countryside and smoke all through the air. Luckily we were at the beach, so we could all go swimming and stay cool. My mom and dad and Richard had been invited to have lunch at a fancy château and they wanted me to go with them. "Are you kidding?" I said. "It's the hottest day of the year!"

"Fanny, it's a once-in-a-lifetime experience," my dad said.

"Château d'Yquem is one of the oldest winemakers in France," Richard said. "They made wine for Louis XIV and Napoleon and Thomas Jefferson. Even writers like Alexandre Dumas, who wrote *The Three Musketeers*."

"You might like it," my mom said. "The wine is sweet."

My mom finally came up with the idea that got me to go. Right before we got into the car, we all put on our bathing suits and went swimming in the ocean. We got really cooled off. Then instead of putting on our fancy clothes, we just took them in the car with us. And we drove to the *château* in our bathing suits—with all the windows wide open. It was so much fun! None of us got hot!

When we got close to the *château*, my dad pulled the car over behind some vines. We all changed out of our bathing suits and into our clothes. I'm so glad we did, because, when we drove up to the front door of the *château*, Richard's friend, the count, was really dressed up.

The count was really nice. His house had so many rooms in it; some were even in round towers. The dining room had a really long table in the middle of it and there were huge fancy lights hanging from the ceiling. There were so many forks and spoons and knives and plates and glasses on the table, I didn't know what to do. All I could think as we sat down was, *How am I supposed to eat with all these things? I don't want to make a mistake.*

"Just copy me," Richard said quietly out of the side of his mouth. "I'll show you how."

During the whole lunch I watched Richard and I copied whatever he did. When he picked up a little spoon, I did too. When he picked up the glass on the right side, so did I. I picked up exactly the same fork or spoon or glass or knife that Richard did when each course came. There were a lot of courses, and each course had a different glass of wine to try. I just got sips. My mom was right, though. The wine was very sweet and it tasted good on a hot day. I told the count this in my best French, and it made him really happy. He even asked me if I wanted to go swimming in his pool after lunch.

"I just happen to have my bathing suit!" I said.

One time I went to visit my friends Maud and Elsa. Their dad, Jean-Pierre, is the chef at Chez Panisse. He and their mom, Denise, are from Bordeaux, so they all go there to live in the summer. When I got to their house, Jean-Pierre asked if Maud and Elsa and I wanted to help him make a *mirepoix*.

"*Mirepoix?*" I said. "What's that?"

It turns out a *mirepoix* is a special mixture of carefully chopped vegetables and herbs that French people use to start lots of things they cook. Jean-Pierre was going to use a *mirepoix* to make braised duck legs.

"Sounds hard," I said.

"Not if you get your *mise en place* together first, Fanny," Jean-Pierre said. "If you organize things before you start, anything you cook is *très facile!*"

I wasn't so sure, but I decided to help anyway. First Jean-Pierre got out little bowls and put one down in front of each of us. Then he gave each of us our own vegetable and asked us to cut it up. "The secret to a good *mirepoix*," Jean-Pierre said, "is to get everything the same size so that everything cooks evenly." Maud carefully diced the celery, and Elsa chopped the carrots into little cubes. I tried to dice the onions exactly the same size. It was so hard, because the onions were making me cry as I cut them.

After the vegetables were chopped, we put them in a bowl. "*Parfait!*" Jean-Pierre said. "Now step two."

He took us outside and we all picked some herbs from his garden. I got some thyme, Elsa cut some parsley, and Maud picked a few bay leaves. We brought all these inside and Jean-Pierre tied them together with string and made a *bouquet garni*, which is just what it sounds like: a bouquet of herbs.

"*Voilà!*" Jean-Pierre exclaimed. "Now, the last step—putting it all together in a pan with some butter."

Jean-Pierre was right. When you put things in order first, it's not that hard. I really learned how to cook like a great chef that day. We must've made a great *mirepoix*, because everyone who came into the kitchen said, "It sure smells good!"

The best oysters I've ever had were wild ones that Jean-Pierre got right out of the waters of the Bassin d'Arcachon, a beautiful sheltered bay in Bordeaux. We got up really early one morning just as the tide was going out. We got into Denise's father's *pinasse,* which is a beautiful flat-bottomed wooden boat that you have to use in the *bassin* because the tides rise and fall so quickly.

We sailed out through all the oyster farm stakes sticking out of the water until we got way beyond them. I asked Jean-Pierre why we didn't just get oysters from one of the farms, and he said, "They're good, but we're looking for better—*huîtres sauvages*!" And then, suddenly, he jumped into the shallow water, held his breath, and disappeared under the surface.

When Jean-Pierre came back up, he had what looked like a pile of messy mud in one of his hands. But when he washed the mud off, we saw that underneath were a bunch of wild oysters all stuck to some rocks and to each other.

We helped Jean-Pierre climb back into the boat, and right away he pulled out his pocketknife. He gently and carefully pried the oysters open, one by one. He made it look so easy to do, but I know it wasn't. Jean-Pierre gave us each our own oyster to taste and it was amazing—salty and plump with tons of juice.

We were so happy sitting out in the boat eating oysters that we lost track of time. But when we started to turn the boat around, we

found we couldn't move! The
tide had gone out and there was no water
underneath the boat anymore. We were stuck!

"*Pas de problème!*" Denise said. "We'll have lunch while we wait for
the tide to come in!"

Denise pulled out some baskets that were full of cheeses and
saucissons, tomatoes, radishes, olives, fruit, and country bread. We
all sat around the huge wooden table built right into the middle of
the boat and had a picnic. We toasted *la mer, le poisson, l'huître*, and,
of course, Jean-Pierre. And sure enough, by the time we were done
eating, the tide had come back in and we could sail right back to shore.

*O*ne spring we went with Maud, Elsa, Jean-Pierre, and Denise to see how a shepherd made cheese. But the shepherd lived so far up in the Pyrenees mountains that we had to hike for over four hours to get there, and then stay overnight in tents.

The shepherd's hut was in the most beautiful valley, under huge mountain peaks that still had snow on them. When we got there, we could see the sheep grazing way up on the mountain. They looked like little white dots of cotton in the middle of a million wildflowers. The shepherd—whose name was André— said we could set up our tents anywhere near his hut. Maud and Elsa and I picked a good spot near a rock for our tent.

As the sun started to go down, we heard the loudest whistle ever. It was André. He was whistling so loudly that it echoed all through the mountain peaks. When his two dogs heard André's whistle, they stopped playing with us and ran like bullets straight up the mountain to the sheep. André kept whistling, and every time he whistled the dogs changed direction. My dad said André was guiding the dogs with his whistle. And my dad was right, because as we watched the dogs go back and forth following Andre's whistles, they started to gather the sheep together and bring them down the mountain. The dogs had to be really careful and try really hard not to leave any sheep behind.

When the sheep got down to us, André opened a little gate in a stable area and all the sheep trotted in. André asked if anybody wanted to help milk the sheep. *"Bien sûr!"* we all said, even though none of us knew how to do it. It didn't matter, because André showed us all how to reach under the smelly sheep's bellies and squeeze their udders so

One by one, the shepherd milks his sheep by hand.

the milk came out. It was weird and hard to do at first, but then we got used to it. It took a while—and our fingers got tired—but with all of us helping, we finally got all the sheep milked. There was so much milk! I think every sheep had over a gallon inside it! It's kind of amazing—the sheep eat grass and we get milk!

The shepherd pours the fresh warm milk into a metal milk can.

The shepherd cools the full milk cans in an ice-cold mountain stream.

He carries the cold milk to his hut.

That night we helped Jean-Pierre cook a big dinner for everyone under the stars. We ate at a big table made from a mountain boulder and sang shepherd songs André knew. When it was time to go to bed, we went inside our tents and turned on our flashlights. The tents all looked like lanterns glowing on the mountainside.

The next day we woke up to the clanging of bells and the *baa*-ing of

sheep. We looked outside our tents and saw the dogs leading the sheep back up the mountain to their grazing pastures. *"Au revoir!"* we said to the sheep as they went by.

Before breakfast, we watched André make his special cheese. First he lit a fire and poured all the sheep's milk we'd gathered the night before into a big copper pot. Then André put the pot on the fire and kept stirring the milk patiently with his hands as it heated up. After a while, the cheese started to form in his fingers like pale yellow clay. And then, suddenly, like magic, the clay turned into a huge blob of soft cheese that André pulled out of the liquid! He set the cheese in a pail nearby where it could cool down and get solid. Wow!

After that, André made another kind of cheese from the liquid that was still left in the pot. He kept heating that up until little solid things rose to the top like hard bubbles. When there were lots of these hard bubbles, Andre scooped them up with a big wooden spoon. My mom said this was *fromage frais*, and we all got to eat some for breakfast. It was still warm and tasted so good (especially with the jam made from rosebuds that André had made from a recipe his grandmother had given him). My mom said it was the most delicious breakfast she'd ever had.

P.S. The French word for cheese is *fromage*.

He heats the milk over a gas burner, stirring and watching the temperature.

The curds and whey separate when the milk reaches the right temperature. By stirring with his hand, the shepherd helps this process.

The curds come together, forming a soft block of cheese.

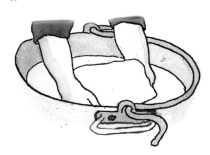

The shepherd wraps the cheese in fresh white cheesecloth and allows it to drain further.

The block drains in a colander. The shepherd pokes iron needles into it to help the cheese drain.

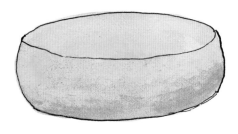

The finished cheese as it looks months later.

$\mathcal{D}$o you know what *les grenouilles* means? It means "frogs." And they eat frogs' legs in France! I'm not kidding. I even ate them once at a fancy restaurant in the Loire Valley called La Maison Troisgros.

Troisgros sounds like it means "three big guys," so I was expecting this house where giants lived. But instead it was a pretty restaurant run by a nice father and son whose last name was Troisgros. Pierre and Michel did wear giant white hats when they cooked, so maybe that's where their name came from. They were so nice. They even took me into the huge kitchen, which was really busy, with lots of other chefs wearing giant white hats. Everyone was making the most amazing-looking and amazing-smelling things.

Back at our table, Pierre said, "*Alors*, now I want to bring you the specialty of the house!" And guess what that was? *Les grenouilles!* I didn't even think I could eat frogs' legs, but the Troisgros were standing there, so what was I supposed to do? But you know what? I took a little bite and they were good. They didn't really even taste "froggy." They eat snails in France too. I've had those and they're good, especially with lots of garlic and parsley butter. And you know what? When people come from France to visit me in Berkeley, they can't believe I eat corn on the cob—they think that only pigs eat corn that way. I guess everybody eats different things in different places.

After dinner, the Troisgros brought the most amazing dessert cart I'd ever seen to our table. There were so many things on it, I couldn't believe they all fit. There were apple tarts, *tuiles à l'orange*, white peaches in jelly, figs in *sabayon*, an almond cake, and hot *soufflés*! It was so hard to decide. But I chose the *brochette de fruits*—which was a shish kebab made with fruit. *Fantastique!*

Our friend Susie likes to rent big houses so all her friends can come stay with her and have fun. Once, she rented this big house in the woods near Bergerac that she said was over two hundred years old. I believe it! All the furniture was really old, and the wooden floors creaked when you walked across them. The bed I slept in was huge and had a canopy over it that was striped red and white just like a candy cane. It was really nice except the mattress was so worn down on both sides that there was a huge hump in the middle. I think it might even have been made out of straw! When I tried to go to sleep, I always felt like I was falling off one side of a mountain or another. I kept thinking that the people who slept in the bed before me must not have liked each other very much!

The house was in the middle of nowhere, and even though there were other kids around, I didn't know what we were going to do. There was no TV or DVD player or Internet. But Susie always says, "There are little wonders everywhere. You just have to know how to look for them." So we started looking—and we found some!

In the field next to the house, there were giant, rolled-up haystack wheels. We all helped each other climb to the top of them and then rolled down the sides. It was so much fun. Even Gracie, Susie's dog, did it with us!

Then we found an old swimming pool that was filled by water from a stream. The water flowed in one end of the pool and out the other, so the water stayed really clear and clean all the time. Nico came up with the idea of putting a swing in a tree branch over the pool. That was really fun too! *Splash!*

Then Susie asked if we wanted to go on a treasure hunt in the woods. I said I was kind of afraid because the woods looked dark and scary. But Susie said, "Don't worry. Gracie will protect us." (Which was funny, because Gracie is about as big as a squirrel.) Susie also said, "When you know the names of the trees and flowers, they become like friends and you don't need to be afraid of them." So as we walked, Susie pointed out chestnut trees and elm trees and pine trees. She also told us the names of flowers and plants like periwinkle and myrtle. Susie said these were the treasures we were looking for on our hunt, and they were beautiful! Katie and Jackie found some wild mushrooms, and we got so excited. We asked Susie's friend Mona, who's a mushroom expert and a cook, if they were mushrooms we could eat. Mona said yes, so we picked the mushrooms to take back to the house. Then I saw something I recognized from back home—wild mint. And I picked some of that!

When we got back to the house, it was getting dark. Since there was no electricity, we lit candles in every room. Monique had the idea of making shadow animals on the wall with our hands. We did that and then we made up whole plays with our hand shadows.

Mona cooked a big *soupe au pistou* over the fire. And while we waited for it to get hot, she grilled the mushrooms Katie and Jackie had found. We put those on toast and they were so good! We all ate in the old dining room just like it was two hundred years ago.

After dinner, I made a *tisane*, a hot tea, just the way my mom taught me, using the wild mint I'd found in the forest! Everyone liked it. I even showed my mom's friend Brigitte, who had a cold, how to use it to make herself feel better. You put a napkin over your head and get under it with the *tisane* and then you breathe in the warm minty steam. I think it worked, because Brigitte stayed under that napkin for a while.

After dinner, we chased fireflies through the trees outside until we were all dead tired. All of us, that is, except Gracie.

I've never been so homesick as I was the time I went to France with my school. I was eight years old, and we all stayed with different families. It was the first time I'd ever been away from home without my mom and dad, and I was gone for two whole weeks!

Luckily my French family was really nice. Their last name was Boncoeur, and they lived in a huge apartment building with a clangy elevator, just outside of Paris in a place called Puteaux. Madame Boncoeur did everything she could to make me feel at home. One night, she saw me reading with my flashlight in the bedroom I shared with her daughters, Celeste and Marie-Laure. Instead of getting mad, Madame Boncoeur bought me a little headlamp so I could wear it under the covers and read and not wake anyone up. Another time, she saw how much I was choking because her husband smoked all the time in the apartment. So Madame Boncoeur gave me a little bandana I could tie around my nose and mouth when I was in the apartment. She also made me a little patchwork market bag out of fabric scraps so I could take my books to school and look like the French kids.

My mom says it's okay to eat some things with your hands, but the Boncoeurs used a knife and fork for everything. They even ate pizza with a knife and fork! It wouldn't have been so bad except everyone in the family had his or her own napkin that they kept folded neatly on the backs of their chairs when they weren't eating. This was so everyone could use the same napkin more than once without having to wash it. Well, after most dinners, everyone's napkin was really clean. Everyone's, that is, but mine. Because I sometimes ate with my hands, my napkin was a total mess! But instead of saying anything mean, Madame Boncoeur just quietly washed my napkin every night and hung it up to dry for the next day. I was kind of ashamed to see my napkin—and nobody else's—hanging up in the apartment every day.

Even though Madame Boncoeur and her family were so nice, I still couldn't stop crying at night and missing home. Madame Boncoeur asked me, "What do you and your mother do when you're back home? Maybe we can do something like that and help you feel better?" I thought about it for a moment and said, "Well, we like to walk in the garden and smell flowers. And we like to listen to music and dance. And we like to cook together."

"J'ai une idée!" Madame Boncoeur exclaimed. She pulled a stool up next to her in the kitchen and handed me a little knife and some garlic. "Tonight you peel the garlic!"

I sat in the kitchen and peeled clove after clove of garlic while Madame Boncoeur prepared the rest of the dinner. At one point, Madame Boncoeur looked over at me and saw I had a huge pile of garlic in front of me. "Fanny!" she said. "That's a lot of garlic! You must like it!"

"My mom says, 'Garlic is as good as ten mothers,'" I told her.

"Well, your mom must be Provençal if she likes garlic that much!" Madame Boncoeur responded.

That night all the Boncoeurs really liked their dinner. So I started helping Madame Boncoeur in the kitchen a lot. And you know what? Suddenly I wasn't crying and missing home so much. I think Madame Boncoeur liked it too, because she started cooking old family recipes she hadn't cooked in a long time, like *boeuf bourguignon*. The most delicious thing Madame Boncoeur made was a *potage de cresson*—a watercress soup. She had to go to a special farmers' market to get the watercress. And she made it just like her mother had showed her when she was a little girl—with potatoes and garlic and fine herbs. I had five helpings!

P.S. You know what *Boncoeur* means in French? It means "good heart."

$\mathscr{I}$ always want to eat bread in France, but my mom won't let me eat just any bread. It has to be "real bread" that comes from what she calls a "real bakery." To my mom, a "real bakery" is one that makes its own dough—usually just out of water, organic flour, and salt—and one that takes the time to let the bread rise naturally before cooking. A "*really real bakery*," according to my mom, is one where the bread is made by hand and baked in a wood-fired oven. "Good bread is the staff of life!" she always says.

Monsieur Poilâne feels the same way about bread that my mom does. "*Le pain est la culture!*" he says. He only makes bread the traditional way. Maybe that's why his bakery, on a little street in Paris, is always really crowded. Or maybe it's because all the bread at Monsieur Poilâne's looks amazing and smells even better! One time, I was about to pick a pretty loaf of *pain au levain* to eat for lunch when Monsieur Poilâne came up to me and said, "*Un moment!* I think I have something you'll like better downstairs!"

Downstairs? I wondered.

Monsieur Poilâne smiled and motioned me to follow him through a little door. We climbed down these old stone stairs that were so steep, I was afraid I might slip! The lower we went, the hotter it got. I saw why when we got to the bottom: the whole basement was taken up by a huge brick bread oven! And in the oven was a gigantic crackling fire. It was so hot down there that all the bakers were wearing T-shirts and shorts! And they were all covered with flour and they were busy throwing wood into the fire. And at the same time, they were putting in and pulling out loaves of bread! It was crazy!

Monsieur Poilâne borrowed a big wooden spatula from one of the bakers. He slid the spatula in through the oven door and after a moment he pulled out a kid-size bubbling apple tart. *"Bon appétit,"* he said. I blew on the tart and took a bite. And then another . . . and then another . . . and before you knew it, that tart was gone!

Bastille Day in Paris! July fourteenth! You walk around the city and everybody's happy. There are flags and celebrations everywhere. All the parks are full and you always hear someone saying *"Vive la France!"*

Our friends Randal and David, who have an old apartment with two fireplaces, usually cook a big dinner for Bastille Day, and I got to help them once. We walked to a market that was right near the Bastille—that's the old jail where the French Revolution started. Arturo, their dog, went with us too, because Arturo goes everywhere with Randal and David—even on airplanes! It's fun to walk around Paris with Arturo because he looks at everything, but he does have to stop and smell every tree and post and flower and step, so it can be kind of slow.

The market on the rue d'Aligre was so busy. There were tons of people out shopping, and French flags were on every stall. David said we should walk through the whole market before deciding what to buy. I remember ducks and chickens and eggs and fennel and fish and these great big scallops in giant seashells called *coquilles Saint-Jacques* and cheese and bread and lettuces and radishes and pastries. My nose was spinning from all the smells, and my ears were spinning from all the sounds of people selling things. There was even a man selling orange footbath powder who was sitting with his feet in a tub of orange water! There were so many people that Randal had to carry Arturo in his arms so he wouldn't get stomped on! I was thinking, *How are we ever going to decide what to make?* Then David introduced me to a nice man from Morocco who was selling beautiful vegetables from piles of tomatoes and fennel and eggplant and zucchini. He had big bunches of mint, too—it smelled so good! David said, "Puts me in mind of couscous."

"Sounds good," Randal said. Then Arturo barked (but I think he was just barking at another dog he saw).

We bought all the things we needed for couscous and then we went back to their apartment. I helped David chop all the vegetables while he baked a chicken stuffed with forty cloves of garlic. Randal set a long table in the other room while Arturo, who was tired from the walk, just lay on his favorite chair, watching.

When friends started to arrive, David pulled a special couscous pot down from a shelf and started steaming the couscous. He let me toast some spices on the stove next to him. The spices smelled so good, I started to get hungry. David gave me some cucumber dipped in yogurt to hold me over until dinner.

After the couscous was steamed, my mom poured it all into a
big pile on a huge platter. Then we put the vegetables we'd chopped
and cooked around it. David let me sprinkle some cinnamon on top.
He pulled the garlicky chicken out of the oven and put that with the
couscous too. I asked him if there was something to put on top of the
chicken, and David said, "Maybe some pepper?" So I got to use the big
pepper grinder!

Randal opened a bottle of champagne, and everyone toasted
the French Revolution. After dinner, the table was such a mess
that we all helped clear it before we had dessert. Then we had a

fruit *macédoine* that had lots of my favorite fruits in it. It tasted especially great because my mom put some rose petal jam in it that Pat and Walter had brought. And because it was the most important French holiday, Camille, who I've known ever since I was a baby, brought one of Randal's and my most favorite French desserts—*macarons*! All different colors! I couldn't help giving Arturo one!

P.S. Randal and David used to have another dog, named Ajax. Ajax was even crazier than Arturo. That's why they called their apartment *Aux Chiens Lunatiques,* which means "with the crazy dogs." But I'm never really sure if David and Randal mean their dogs are the crazy ones or if they are. . . .

*O*nce, Camille took us to the biggest picnic ever. She said all of France was getting together to celebrate on the same day at the same time! They were putting a huge tablecloth across the whole country so that everyone, no matter where they lived, could have a place at the table! The Paris tablecloth went right through the Luxembourg Gardens, and that's where we went.

There were so many people when we got there; I saw jugglers and opera singers and puppeteers and magicians and *pétanque* players and French soldiers and people dressed like it was the 1700s and soccer players playing soccer. And I saw birds peeking out of the holes of the special birdhouses that are on poles in the park. And there were so many kids running around—up and down all the trails between the trees and the fountains and the statues. There was even a little orchestra playing in a gazebo.

We found a place right near the apple and pear orchards. This made my mom so happy, because you could see the fruit on the trees. You could also see the bees buzzing around the tree branches and then flying back to the hives the park had made for them. "*Regarde*, Fanny! They're making honey!" my mom said. "Right above our heads! Right in the middle of Paris!" We all wished we could have some of that honey.

We squeezed in between lots of other people eating lots of different things. There were people next to us from Brittany who were eating oysters. The family across from us was from Normandy, and they were eating apples and duck *rillettes*. On the other side of them were some college students eating falafel and drinking beer. Near them were some farmers eating ham sandwiches and eggs dipped in mayonnaise, and they were drinking wine out of bottles that had no labels on them.

And further down there were people all dressed up in fancy clothes with candles in front of them, drinking champagne and eating lobster salad!

I helped Camille put our plates and silverware out. David and Randal and Arturo showed up and they had some flowers in a wine bottle. I put those in the middle of our spot. That was pretty! They had some radishes and salt, too. Yum! Camille and my mom had packed lots of good things to eat. There were olives and *cornichons* and *mesclun* salad and tomatoes and hard-boiled eggs and even some little sardines. Laurence came out of the crowd, carrying a big bottle of Lulu and Lucien's wine. My dad opened that right away. He even shared some with the people next to us! Then our friend Peggy found us. She said that even though she lived right near the park, she'd gotten totally lost! She brought special red, blue, and white napkins, and I put those around so our place looked really French. Peggy also brought her favorite thing—five different kinds of cheeses.

It was so much fun, and we shared everything we had with everyone around us.

In the middle of lunch, the mayor of Paris stood on a balcony and made a speech. He said, "In France eating is togetherness." The whole park raised a glass to that! *Salut!*

Salad Flowers

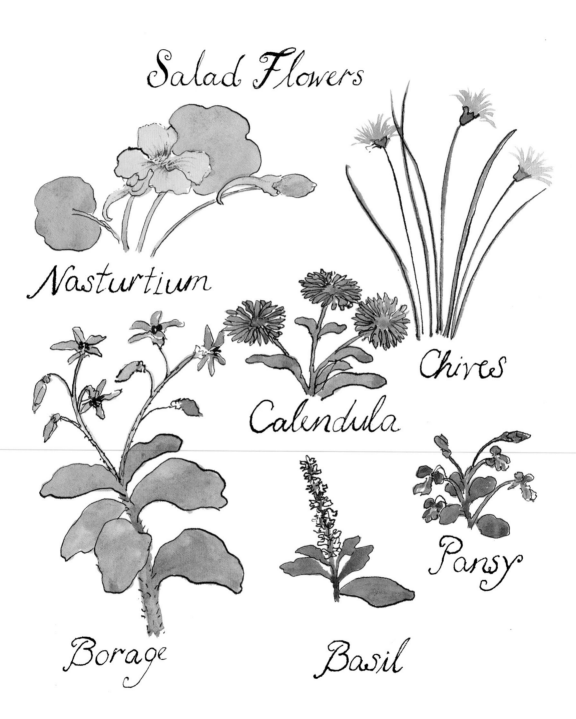

Nasturtium

Chives

Calendula

Borage

Basil

Pansy

Fanny's French Recipes

These are some of my favorite things I learned to cook in France. Maybe they'll become your favorites too!

MY MOM'S SPECIAL "FRENCH" RULES

My mom has learned some very important things about cooking and food from her friends in France. She's taught them to me, and I want to share them with you:

❧ Shop at farmers' markets—they're the places where the food is most alive and tasty. Plus, you get to meet the people who grow your food and learn how they do it.

❧ Plant a garden—even if it's just a pot of herbs in a window. It makes cooking—and where you live—way better.

❧ Economize—which means don't buy too much or eat too much. You'll be surprised how a little can go a long way.

❧ Balance your menu—which means eat lots of different things rather than just one or two things.

❧ Treasure the past—look for beautiful and well-made things in flea markets and secondhand stores.

❧ Ask for help—it's fun to learn from other cooks. Plus, if you need to use a sharp knife or a hot oven or stove—or even an electric blender or mixer—it's good to have an adult show you the safest way.

❧ Set the table—even if your table is a counter or a floor or a picnic blanket! And start each meal with a toast. *Salut!*

By the way, you can use whole-wheat flour in this recipe. If you want to do that, use the same amount of flour but make half of it whole-wheat and half of it all-purpose flour.

Now you're ready to make the dough into bread! (You can keep the dough in the refrigerator for a day or two before you form it and bake it.)

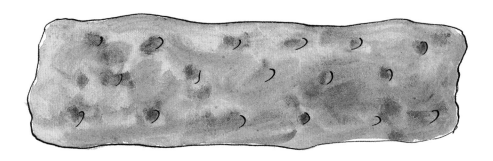

Flatbread

Makes 1 loaf

This is the easiest bread to make. It makes a round flat loaf that's about 1 inch thick. My mom cuts squares out of it, then slices them up and makes sandwiches that are crispy on both sides. Yum!

> 1 dough recipe
>
> Olive oil
>
> Flaky sea salt

Lightly oil a sheet pan and sprinkle a little flaky sea salt on it. Then, with your hands moistened with olive oil, scrape the dough out of the bowl and plop it onto the pan in a mound. The dough will be a bit crazy and spread all over the place. Just use your hands to gently tuck under any scraggly ends. Spread a little more olive oil on top of the dough and then gently push the dough down and shape it into a disk about ½ inch thick and 1 foot across. Salt the top with more flaky sea salt. Then lightly press the surface of the bread down in different places with your fingertips to create little dimples. Let the dough rest for **15** minutes. Bakers call this "proofing."

Preheat the oven to **500**° F. After the bread is proofed, bake on the center rack of the oven for **12** minutes. You'll know the bread is done when it is a light golden brown and sounds hollow when you tap it with your finger.

Remove the flatbread from the oven and let it cool on a rack. Now you're ready to make sandwiches.

Baguettes

*Makes three **12**-inch-long baguettes*

1 dough recipe

If you want to make baguettes, follow the flatbread recipe, but when you get to the part where you've plopped down your dough onto the baking sheet, instead of pressing it flat, cut the dough into **3** equal pieces. Form each of these pieces into a long loaf by rolling and stretching the dough. You should end up with **3** loaves that are about **12** inches long and about **2** inches thick. Line up the loaves next to each other on the sheet pan, but leave enough space between them so they don't touch. Let the loaves proof for **20** minutes.

Preheat the oven to **500°** F and bake the loaves the same way you do flatbread. You'll know the baguettes are done when they're brown on the top and on the bottom and they make a hollow sound when you knock your finger against them. Let the baguettes cool on a rack, and then—*mangez*!

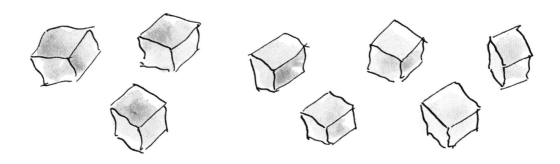

Croûtons

Croûtons are little crusty toasts that you put in soups or salads. My mom likes to put garlic and olive oil on them because she likes to put garlic and olive oil on everything!

Baguettes, flatbread, or any other good plain bread
1 garlic clove
Olive oil

Preheat the oven to **400°** F. Slice the bread into ⅓-inch-thick slices and put them on a baking sheet. Toast for **8** minutes or so, until the outsides are brown. Cut a garlic clove in half. Rub the garlic on the hot toast and drizzle with olive oil.

Bread Crumbs

If you have more bread than you can eat while it's still fresh, when it's a day or two old, make bread crumbs. If you have a leftover 12-inch-long baguette, for example, it will make around 1 cup of bread crumbs.

Yesterday's bread

Preheat the oven to 300° F. Cut the crust off the bread. Then tear the bread into roughly 1-inch pieces and put them on a sheet pan. Put the pan in the oven for 25 minutes or so, until the bread dries out. You don't want it really toasted; you want it dry and lightly colored, kind of "almost toasted." Let the bread cool completely. Using a grater, a mortar and pestle, or a food processor, grind the bread into fine but not too tiny crumbs. The crumbs can be made in advance and stored in an airtight container until needed.

Hors d'Oeuvres

In French, *hors d'oeuvre* means "outside the work," and *hors d'oeuvres* are little things you make to eat outside of the main event, before you sit down to the meal or while you're still cooking—or sometimes, just little snacks. They're really just little nibbles.

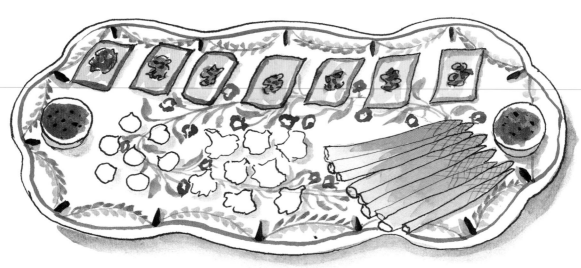

Tapenade

François's Marinated Olives

*Makes **4** servings*

You can use any kind of olive you want, but I like green olives like Lucques or Picholine the best. The outer colored part of lemon peel (and the peel of other citrus fruits too, like limes and oranges) is called the zest. You can use a vegetable peeler (the kind with a blade that swivels) to make paper-thin strips that are all zest, with none of the inner white part of the peel (or only a little).

- 1 cup olives
- 2 to 3 long strips of lemon zest
- ¼ teaspoon fennel seeds
- 2 or 3 thyme sprigs, torn into 1-inch pieces
- 1 tablespoon olive oil

Take the olives out of their brine. Put the olives into a sauté pan and toss with the lemon zest, fennel seeds, thyme, and olive oil. Warm the marinated olives gently over low heat for **3** minutes. Spoon into a bowl. When you serve them, make sure you put another small dish nearby for the pits.

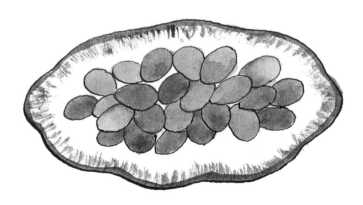

Slow-Roasted Almonds with Sage Leaves

Makes about 2 ½ cups

Roasting almonds with sage at a low temperature makes the almonds toasty and the sage crispy. Plus it makes the whole house smell good when you do it! The only trick is to watch the almonds carefully, because after about a half hour, they'll go from golden to burnt in just a few minutes.

- 2 cups almonds
- 1 cup sage leaves, loosely packed (about 1 large bunch)
- 2 tablespoons olive oil
- ½ teaspoon sea salt

Preheat the oven to 275° F. On a sheet pan, mix together the almonds and sage leaves. Add the olive oil and salt. Toss gently until the nuts and sage are evenly coated. Spread the nuts evenly on the sheet pan and bake in the preheated oven, stirring every now and then.

After about 20 minutes, scoop out a few nuts with a spoon and cut them open with a small knife. If they are golden brown in the center, they are done. If their insides are still white, put the pan back into the oven, checking again after 5 more minutes. You want the nuts to roast fully, but not to burn. I usually find 35 minutes or so does the trick.

Remove from the oven and let cool on the pan. Serve in a pretty bowl.

Oeuf Mayonnaise

Makes 1 serving

This means "egg mayonnaise" and it's very simple to make. And it's really good. Making your own mayonnaise takes some practice, but once you get it, you'll always want to make your own. My mom told me a great secret about making mayonnaise: before you start, make sure the egg is at room temperature. If the egg is right out of the refrigerator, I put it in a bowl of very warm water for **5** to **10** minutes.

For the hard-cooked egg:

> 1 egg, at room temperature

For the mayonnaise (makes about 1 cup):

> 1 egg, at room temperature
> Sea salt
> 1 cup light olive oil
> ¼ teaspoon vinegar or lemon juice

For the oeuf mayonnaise:

> 3 tablespoons homemade mayonnaise
> Sea salt
> Fresh-ground black pepper
> Chervil and chives to garnish

Chives

Chervil

First hard-cook the egg:

(My mom doesn't like to say "hard-boiled egg," because you don't really boil it; you barely even simmer it!) Fill a small pot with water and bring it to a boil. Turn down the heat to a simmer and add the egg to the pot with a spoon. While the egg is simmering very gently, fill a bowl big enough for the egg with ice water. After **8** minutes, turn off the heat, remove the egg from the pan, and put it in the ice water to chill.

Then make the mayonnaise:

First you need to separate the yolk and the white of the uncooked egg. You can do this by holding your hand over a small bowl and cracking the egg open into your hand. Let the egg white slip through your fingers into the bowl while you keep the yolk in your hand. Put the yolk in a medium-size bowl. Set aside the egg white to use for something else. (You can refrigerate raw egg whites for several days.) Season the yolk with a good pinch of salt and set the bowl on a damp towel so it won't slip and slide.

Measure the olive oil into a container with a pour spout. With a whisk, mix the egg yolk and salt together with a few drops of warm water. Slowly—and I mean slowly!—begin to add the oil to the egg, at first drop by drop, whisking all the time. You'll see the egg yolk start to thicken gradually as it absorbs the oil. If you add too much oil at once, the egg and oil will stay separate. You need them to come together at the very start or the mayonnaise won't work. So it is good to go slowly and be patient.

After you've mixed in about ¼ cup of oil, the mayonnaise will start to get thick. If it gets too thick, you can thin it by adding ½ teaspoon of warm water. Then continue to whisk in the oil in a thin, steady stream until all the oil is added.

Finish the mayonnaise by seasoning it: add about ¼ teaspoon of lemon juice and salt to taste. If you're not going to use it right away, keep the mayonnaise chilled in the refrigerator.

Now you're ready to put the oeuf mayonnaise *together:*

When the hard-cooked egg is cool, peel the shell off and cut the egg in half lengthwise. Put the egg on a pretty plate, yolk side down. Spoon a big spoonful of the mayonnaise over the egg. Sprinkle with chopped chives or chervil. *Voilà!*

Crudités

Makes 6 servings

Crudités is a French word for raw vegetables. You can cut them any way you want, but I like to cut the vegetables so they keep their natural shape. You'll see when you put the vegetables in salted ice water for a few minutes, they crisp up and some even curl! Besides these vegetables, you can use any tender ones you find or grow, like young turnips, little green beans (*haricots verts* in French), or my favorite, the first fava beans of spring.

1 celery heart (the tender, inner stalks from a bunch of celery)

1 large carrot

1 bunch radishes, the French breakfast variety, if available

5 cups water

2 cups ice cubes

1 teaspoon salt

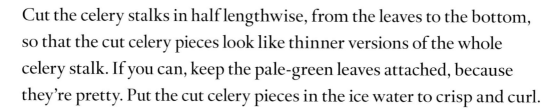

Wash all of the vegetables and put them on a cutting board. Put about 5 cups of water and 2 cups of ice cubes in a medium-size bowl. Stir in the salt.

Cut the celery stalks in half lengthwise, from the leaves to the bottom, so that the cut celery pieces look like thinner versions of the whole celery stalk. If you can, keep the pale-green leaves attached, because they're pretty. Put the cut celery pieces in the ice water to crisp and curl.

Peel the outer skin off the carrot with a vegetable peeler. Still using the vegetable peeler and pressing harder this time, hold the carrot at its top and peel again from top to bottom. You'll end up slicing off ribbons of carrot! Keep doing this until there isn't much carrot left. I always like to eat this little leftover portion as a treat. Add the ribbons of carrot to the ice water bath.

Wash the radishes and cut off their stems, leaving a bit of green at the top. If the radishes are too big to serve whole, cut them in half or in quarters. Put the radishes in the ice water.

Once all the vegetables are in the ice water bath, let them sit for 15 minutes. Drain and pat dry on a clean towel. Arrange them on a nice platter with a *vinaigrette* for dipping.

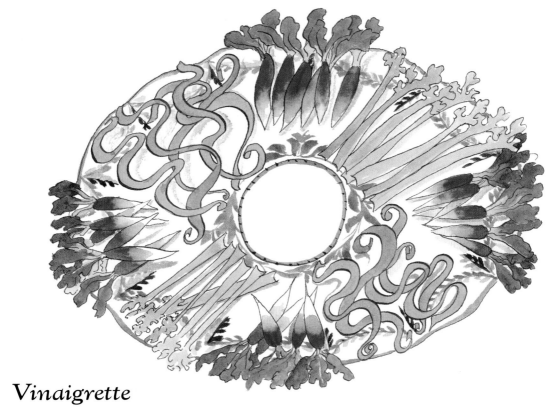

Vinaigrette

Makes about 3 tablespoons

1   small garlic clove

½ to ¾ teaspoon salt

Fresh-ground black pepper

2   teaspoons red wine vinegar

2   tablespoons olive oil

With a mortar and pestle, pound the garlic into a paste with the salt and pepper. Add the vinegar and let this all sit for 5 minutes. Whisk in the olive oil and taste for seasoning, adding more salt and pepper if you think it needs it.

Variations

❧ You can add a teaspoon of Dijon mustard to the *vinaigrette* to make it creamier.

❧ You can make an *aïoli* for a dipping sauce (an *aïoli* is usually just mayonnaise with a lot of garlic in it). Peel 2 small garlic cloves and pound them with a mortar and pestle with a pinch of salt until they turn into a smooth paste. Stir about half the smashed garlic paste into 1 batch of homemade mayonnaise (page 101) and add salt and garlic to taste. If you want to add more, do it, but remember that the longer the garlic sits in the *aïoli*, the stronger it will get!

Gougères (Cheese Puffs)

Makes about 40 small gougères

These are fun to make because they puff up in the oven!

- ½ cup water
- 3 tablespoons butter, cut in small pieces
- ½ teaspoon salt
- ½ cup flour
- 2 eggs
- 3 ounces Gruyère cheese, grated (about ¾ cup)

Preheat the oven to 400° F. In a heavy-bottomed saucepan, heat the water with the butter and salt until the butter has melted. Add all of the flour at one time and stir hard with a wooden spoon until the liquid and the flour are completely mixed together and the mixture pulls away from the sides of the pan. This may take a minute or two, but don't worry; it will come together. Keep stirring for another minute over the heat, then scrape the mixture into a mixing bowl and let it cool slightly.

Beat the eggs into the batter, one at a time, until thoroughly mixed. The batter will look separated at first, but vigorous stirring will make it smooth and even again. Stir in all but ¼ cup of the Gruyère cheese until completely blended.

Line 2 baking sheets with parchment paper. Spoon the dough onto the baking sheets in spoonfuls no bigger than Ping-Pong balls, about 1½ inches apart from each other. The dough will be sticky, so use your finger to help scrape it off the spoon. Sprinkle the remaining cheese on top of each *gougère*. Bake undisturbed for 10 minutes and then lower the temperature to 375° F. Don't open the oven door! Bake for 15 minutes more. The *gougères* should be golden brown and crisp on the outside. Remove them from the oven, and with a sharp pointed knife, poke each warm puff to let out the steam. This will help them to stay crispy. Serve right away!

Gougères

Tapenade

Makes about ½ cup

There are lots of things you can do with *tapenade*. You can spread it on toast or have it with eggs, or put it in some pasta, make a sandwich out of it, or just put it on roasted vegetables. You can use green olives if you don't have black ones.

½ cup black olives (*niçoise* or Nyon)

1 tablespoon capers, rinsed, drained, and coarsely chopped

1 salted anchovy, rinsed in water, filleted, and chopped

1 garlic clove, peeled and pounded to a paste

1 sprig of savory, leaves only, chopped

¼ teaspoon grated lemon zest

¼ cup olive oil

Sea salt (optional)

You need to pit the olives, and you have to be careful, so you might want to ask an adult to help you. Put the olives on a cutting board. Then, using the flat side of a chef's knife (with the knife blade facing away from you), one at a time, firmly press down on each olive until you feel its skin split open a little bit. When all the olives have been split, use your fingers to pull the pit out of each one.

Chop up the pitted olives into very small pieces and put them into a medium-size bowl. Add the capers, chopped anchovy, garlic, savory, lemon zest, and olive oil to the bowl of olives and stir it all together.

Let sit for **30** minutes so that the flavors come together. Taste and, if necessary, add a little salt. Remember, all these ingredients are pretty salty, so you might not need to add any. In fact, sometimes if it is too salty, I add a squeeze of lemon.

Variations

꽃 Add *tapenade* to a grilled mozzarella sandwich or a sliced hard-cooked egg sandwich—yum.

꽃 Thin out the *tapenade* with extra olive oil to make a dressing for cooked vegetables like broccoli, asparagus, or even beets.

Les Potages

Potage is the French word for soup. These are my favorite *potages*—at least for now!

Potage de Cresson (Watercress Soup)

Makes 6 servings

This soup is really green and looks even more amazing when you spoon a little *crème fraîche* on top of it. *Merci*, Madame Boncoeur!

- 3 tablespoons unsalted butter
- 1 white onion, thinly sliced
- 1 leek, white and tender green parts only, halved and thinly sliced
- 1 small garlic clove, minced
- 2 tablespoons parsley, chopped
- Sea salt
- 4 cups water
- 1 potato, peeled, halved, and thinly sliced (about 1 cup)
- 2 bunches watercress (about 5 cups roughly chopped)
- Fresh-ground black pepper
- *Crème fraîche* (optional)

In a medium-size pot, melt the butter over medium heat. Add the onion and leek. Sauté for 5 minutes, or until everything softens. Add the garlic, parsley, and a pinch of salt. Sauté for 1 minute more, stirring a lot so the onion doesn't brown and the garlic doesn't burn. You may need to turn the heat down a bit if the onions start browning.

Add the potato, water, and 2 teaspoons of salt. Bring all this to a boil and then lower the heat to a simmer. Cover and let the liquid simmer for 10 minutes, or until the potato is completely cooked through and breaks apart easily when you poke it with a fork.

Put the watercress in the jar of a blender and ladle the potato mixture over it. Add a little black pepper. Purée the soup, but be careful, because it's really hot and you don't want it to spray out the top of the blender. Sometimes I wrap a towel over the top of the blender just to be safe! Purée until smooth, and then taste for seasoning, adding more salt and pepper if you think it's needed.

To serve, pour the soup back into the pot and reheat it. Then add a spoonful of *crème fraîche*. I promise, you'll be amazed by the colors! And you'll be more amazed by the taste!

Soupe au Pistou

Makes **8** *to* **10** *cups*

Pistou is the French version of the Italian sauce called pesto, a mixture of fresh basil, cheese, and nuts. A spoonful of *pistou* makes any vegetable soup really special. This *pistou* is made without nuts and with just a little cheese, so you can really taste the basil. It may seem like a lot of soup when you make it, but you won't be sorry—it only gets better with time. Here's a little secret: this soup is best when you make it with the liquid that you cooked the beans in.

For the soupe:

- 1 medium-size onion, diced
- 1 large leek, white and tender green parts only, halved and thinly sliced
- 2 medium-size carrots, diced
- 2 tablespoons olive oil
- 1 to 2 garlic cloves, minced

Bouquet garni of 1 celery stalk, 1 thyme branch, 1 parsley branch, and 1 bay leaf

1 medium-size tomato, peeled, seeded, and chopped coarsely

3 cups (14 ounces) butternut squash, cubed

3 small zucchini, thinly sliced or cubed

2 cups cooked flageolet or cannellini beans, cooking liquid reserved (see Beans Cooked over the Fire, page 130)

1 small bunch Swiss chard, washed and stemmed (you can save the stems for another use)

Fresh-ground black pepper

For the pistou:

2 bunches basil, leaves only (4 cups loosely packed leaves)

1 garlic clove

3 tablespoons olive oil

Sea salt

¼ cup grated Parmigiano-Reggiano

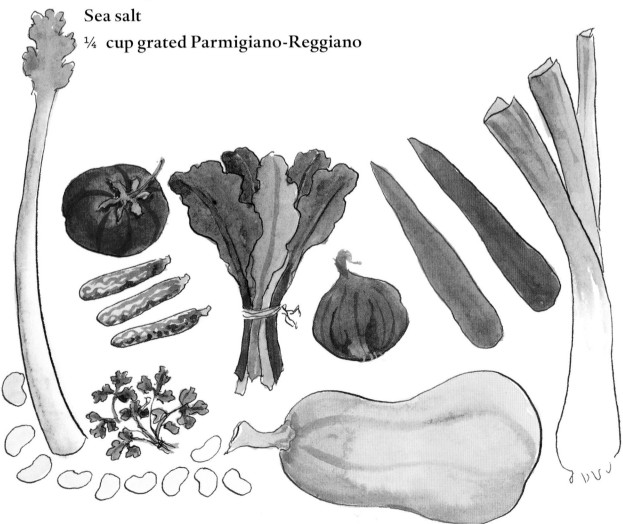

To make the soupe:

Sauté the onion, leek, and carrots in the olive oil in a soup pot over medium-high heat until the onion begins to soften, about **5** minutes. Stir every now and then to make sure the onions don't brown. Add the garlic and cook for **1** minute more.

Pour as much bean liquid as you have into a measuring cup. To that, add enough water to equal **8** cups of liquid in all, pouring it into the soup pot holding the vegetables. Add the *bouquet garni*, tomato, and butternut squash and bring the soup to a boil. Once it boils, lower the heat to a simmer and cook for **15** to **20** minutes, until the squash is tender but not mushy. Add the zucchini and beans and simmer for **10** more minutes. Tear up the Swiss chard leaves and add to the soup. Cover and cook for **5** to **10** minutes, or until the zucchini is completely cooked through. Taste the broth and add more salt and pepper if you like. Remove and discard the *bouquet garni*.

To make the pistou:

Plunging the basil briefly in boiling water makes the *pistou* stay a bright green. (This is called "blanching" or "parboiling.") To do this, bring a small pot of water to a boil. Have a strainer ready in the sink. Drop the basil leaves into the boiling water and right away drain them in the strainer. Then, quickly, pour cold water over them for **10** seconds—shocking them! You don't want the basil leaves to cook— just wake up! Squeeze out the water from the basil leaves, which will have shrunk a lot.

Once dry, blend the basil, garlic, olive oil, and a pinch of salt in the blender or food processor until it becomes a bright-green purée. Add the grated cheese, blend briefly, and then taste for seasoning, adding a touch more salt if needed.

Serve the soup with a spoonful of the *pistou* in the center. I think this soup tastes even better the day after you make it.

Variation

✤ Lots of people add pasta or Arborio rice to *soupe au pistou* to make it more filling. If you want to do this, cook a cup of pasta or rice in salted water until it's barely cooked and still firm, or *al dente*, which is Italian for "to the tooth." That means that when you bite into something, you feel some resistance to your teeth.

Chicken Broth

Makes about 4 quarts

A really good soup can be made from just the bones of chicken—no meat is needed, although the broth will taste better the more meat there is left on the bone. When the bones are simmered in water with a few vegetables, all of the good stuff from the chicken—its flavor, vitamins, and minerals—is released into the water to make a delicious and satisfying broth. This recipe calls for one cooked chicken carcass (the leftover bones and skeleton from a roasted chicken, page **127**), but you can use any chicken parts you want to make the broth. Wings, necks, backs, and even a whole chicken all work.

1 cooked chicken carcass

1 carrot, peeled

1 onion, peeled and halved

1 celery stalk

5 peppercorns

Bouquet garni of 1 bay leaf, 2 thyme branches, and a handful
   of parsley sprigs

Put the chicken carcass in a large pot. Add enough water to cover and bring to a boil. Let it boil gently for **10** to **15** minutes. While it's boiling, use a big flat spoon to skim off the fat and froth that float to the top. When the bubbling broth is nice and clear, add the vegetables, peppercorns, and *bouquet garni*. Lower the heat to a gentle simmer and let the broth simmer for about **2** hours.

Ladle the broth through a fine mesh strainer into large jars or containers. Put in the refrigerator until cold. Once cold, all of the fat from the broth will have floated to the top so it can be easily seen and removed with a spoon. The broth will keep in the refrigerator for up to **4** days, or for months in the freezer. A word of advice: if you are freezing the broth, make sure to fill the container only ¾ full. When the liquid freezes, it expands, and if you've filled the jar too much, it will shatter!

Variation

✤ Try throwing a handful of mushroom stems in the broth for extra flavor. A couple of fennel stalks can be good too, and so can the green top of a leek (cleaned of any dirt, of course!).

Soupe à l'Ail (Garlic Soup)

Makes 2 to 3 servings

My mom says this soup can cure any sickness. It's easy to make and warms you up on a really cold day. It can fill you up even more if you make a toasted *croûton* and drizzle it with a little olive oil. I like to ladle the soup over the *croûton* so it becomes like a soft tasty island in the middle of the broth.

    3 cups chicken broth
    2 garlic cloves, peeled and sliced thinly
    1 thyme sprig
    3 or 4 sage leaves
    Sea salt
    1 teaspoon chopped parsley

Bring the chicken broth to a boil with the garlic, thyme, sage leaves, and a big pinch of salt. Lower to a simmer and remove the sage leaves, as they can get bitter if they're boiled for too long. Simmer for 10 to 15 minutes and taste for seasoning. Add more salt if you think it needs it. Remove the thyme sprig and, just before serving, add the parsley. Serve hot. Ladle the soup into a bowl over a *croûton* (page 96) drizzled with olive oil.

Petits Repas

Petit repas means "a little meal." These are things I make to eat for breakfast or lunch, or if I'm not too hungry at dinner.

Omelet

Makes 1 serving

2 eggs

1 teaspoon water

¼ teaspoon salt

1 tablespoon *fines herbes,* finely chopped (chives, chervil, parsley, and tarragon)

1 tablespoon butter

Crack the eggs into a bowl and add the water, salt, and about ⅔ of the herbs. Beat lightly with a whisk or fork until combined.

You will need a heavy-bottomed nonstick pan that's 6 to 8 inches in diameter (preferably cast-iron). Heat it over medium heat for at least 3 minutes. It's really important to make sure the pan gets hot all over so when you cook the eggs, they won't stick. When the pan is completely hot, add the butter and turn up the heat a little. The butter will quickly melt, sizzle, and foam. As soon as the foaming starts to slow down, pour in the eggs. With a wooden spoon or rubber spatula, push the outer edges of the eggs toward the center as they cook. This will let any uncooked egg in the middle run out onto the hot uncovered parts of the pan. Keep going around the whole omelet, tilting the pan if you need to, to help any uncooked egg run out to touch the pan.

As soon as the egg is nearly cooked, fold one half of the omelet over onto its other half. If it helps, tilt the pan to do this. Place a plate right near the pan and tilt the pan over it so that the omelet rolls onto the plate. Rub a piece of butter over the top of the omelet to make it shiny. Sprinkle with the rest of the herbs. Serve immediately.

Variation

❧ Cheese omelet: sprinkle 1 ounce of grated Gruyère or crumbled goat cheese onto the omelet just as it sets and right before you begin rolling it out of the pan.

Croque-Monsieur (Grilled Cheese Sandwich)

Makes 1 serving

I love grilled cheese sandwiches. This is the version my mom makes me. It's a little less goopy than the French kind. Use good country bread, like a *pain au levain* or whole wheat. In Alsace, they serve a *croque-monsieur* with sauerkraut and pickles. I like to serve it with little *cornichons* and a salad.

2 slices of *levain* or whole-wheat bread
1 ounce (about ¼ cup) aged cow's milk cheese (such as Gruyère, Monterey Jack, or any other tangy cheese), grated
1 thin slice Black Forest ham (or another good dry-cured smoked ham)
Olive oil
1 garlic clove, peeled

Cut **2** slices of bread no more than ⅓-inch thick. Cover **1** slice of bread with half the grated cheese. Put the slice of ham on top and cover with the remaining cheese. Put the other slice of bread on top and brush both sides of the sandwich with olive oil.

Choose a cast-iron pan that's just large enough to hold the sandwich and heat it over medium-low heat for about **2** minutes or until it is heated through. When the pan is hot, put the sandwich in it. Put a smaller heavy pan or lid on top of the sandwich to weigh it down so that it will cook evenly. Cook until golden brown. You can peek by lifting the sandwich up with a spatula. If it is browning too quickly and you think it might burn, turn the heat down a little.

When the bottom slice of bread is toasted and golden, flip the sandwich over and weigh it down again with the small pan. Cook until the other side is golden brown and the cheese inside is melted. When the sandwich is cooked and crisp, remove from the pan and rub a clove of garlic on one side. Cut in half and serve.

Salade Niçoise (Salad from Nice)

*Makes **6** servings*

Lots of times people in Nice make this salad with tuna. But my mom says that these days it's really hard to find good tuna that's been fished the right way. So most of the time we make this salad without tuna, the way Richard made it.

> **1 pound new potatoes**
> **Sea salt**
> **About ½ cup (8 tablespoons) *vinaigrette* (page 105)**

½ pound *haricots verts*
(little green beans), ends
trimmed

½ pound cherry or grape
tomatoes

1 cup loosely packed parsley
leaves

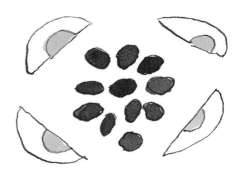

½ cup *niçoise* olives, pitted
and halved

6 ounces tuna, cooked or preserved in oil (optional)

Fresh-ground black pepper

4 hard-cooked eggs (page 102), peeled and quartered

3 salted anchovies, soaked in water, filleted, and cut in strips
(optional)

To cook the potatoes, put them in a large pot with ½ teaspoon of salt. Cover with water and bring to a boil. Lower the heat to a simmer and cook until tender, 15 to 20 minutes, depending on their size. If you can pierce them easily and smoothly with a knife, they are done. Drain the potatoes and let them cool in a colander for a few minutes. Once they are cool enough to handle, peel them, using your fingers to slip off the skins. (You can leave the skins on, if you want.) If the potatoes are larger than a walnut, cut them in half or in quarters. Place the peeled potatoes in a salad bowl and toss them with 4 tablespoons of *vinaigrette.*

Meanwhile, bring another pot of water to a boil and add ½ teaspoon of salt. Add the *haricots verts* and boil them 4 to 7 minutes, until they're tender but still firm. Drain and lay them out in one layer on a sheet pan so they stop cooking and stay green.

Cut the cherry tomatoes in half and coarsely chop the parsley. Add the tomatoes, parsley, and olives to the potatoes. If you are using tuna, now is the time to flake it over the potatoes. Once the *haricots verts* are dry, add them, too. Whisk the rest of the *vinaigrette* and drizzle most of it over the salad. Stir with your hands or a spoon to coat everything evenly. Taste and add more dressing and salt and pepper if you think it needs it. Serve on a platter with the eggs arranged around the outside for a pretty border. Sprinkle a little salt on each quarter of an egg, and if you're using anchovies, drape a strip over each egg.

Variation

✣ If you have leftover *salade niçoise*, do as the Niçoises do and make a *pan bagnat*, which is a sandwich with this salad as a filling.

Pizza with Quick Tomato Sauce

Makes four 9-inch pizzas

The trick to making good pizza dough is not to overwork it. That means when you are stretching the pizza dough, only stretch it and pull it as far as it wants to go and handle it as little as possible.

About 1 cup flour
1 dough recipe (page 92)
One 14-ounce can tomatoes
Olive oil

3½ garlic cloves

A big handful of basil leaves

Sea salt

¼ cup grated aged hard cheese, such as Parmigiano-Reggiano, Asiago, or Pecorino

¾ cup grated mozzarella cheese

3 tablespoons olive oil

Lightly flour a clean flat work surface. Have about a cup more flour ready in a bowl nearby. With a lightly oiled rubber spatula, quickly scrape the inside of the bowl the dough is in to release it. Tilt the bowl toward the floured work surface and push the dough out onto it. Remember, the dough might want to run all over the place, so what I do sometimes is sprinkle a little flour over it to make it less runny and help hold it together.

Using a large knife, divide the dough into 4 pieces. (If the dough sticks to the knife blade, use the oiled spatula to push it off.) Form each piece of dough into a ball and set the balls on a well-floured surface. Let the dough rest for 10 minutes.

While the dough is resting, preheat the oven to 475° F and put a sheet pan in the oven to get hot.

Make a quick tomato sauce: put the tomatoes, olive oil, garlic, and most of the basil leaves in a blender. Blend until puréed, and taste for salt, adding a pinch if you think it needs it.

After the dough has rested and the tomato sauce and grated cheeses are all ready, it is time to make your first pizza: lightly flour your hands, then take one ball of dough and gently pull it. I like to put one hand underneath the dough and pull all along its edges. Remember, pull the dough only as far as it wants to stretch. You don't want to tear or overwork it. Let the dough guide you.

Once you've pulled the dough into a disk shape, let it rest for a minute while you get the hot sheet pan out of the oven. Use oven mitts! Stretch the dough a bit wider, if you can without forcing it. Then transfer the dough to the hot pan, taking care not to touch the hot pan with your hands at all. Spoon a few tablespoons of sauce onto the pizza—just enough to lightly cover the dough, but not so much that you create puddles of it. Leave an inch of uncovered dough around the edge for the crust. Sprinkle the pizza with ¼ cup grated cheese. Then brush around the crust edge lightly with olive oil. Put the pizza in the oven and bake until lightly browned, about **8** minutes. Remove from the oven, cut in wedges, and serve hot topped with a little salt and some of the remaining basil leaves.

Repeat the process with the other dough balls. Store any unused tomato sauce in the refrigerator for up to **5** days.

Plats Principaux

Plats principaux means "main courses." They're a little bit more complicated to make but totally fun and worth it! Get your friends or family to help and it will be even more fun!

Martine's Roast Chicken with Smoked Paprika and Mustard

Makes 6 to 8 servings

1 chicken, 3½ to 4 pounds

Sea salt

2 tablespoons Dijon mustard

Olive oil

1 teaspoon smoked paprika

2 teaspoons thyme, finely chopped

Fresh-ground black pepper

4 to 5 whole garlic cloves, unpeeled

1 lemon, quartered

6 to 8 thyme or savory branches

2 to 3 carrots, peeled and cut in ½-inch slices

3 turnips, peeled, quartered, and cut into ½-inch slices

6 to 8 new potatoes, cut in halves or quarters

The night before cooking the chicken, season it: first, pat the chicken dry, inside and out. Remove any giblets (the heart, the gizzard, and the liver) from the cavity. Sprinkle the whole chicken, inside and out, with 2 to 3 teaspoons of salt. Make sure to salt the back and thighs as well as the breasts. After that, tuck the wing tips up and under the back of the chicken so they don't burn while the chicken cooks. Store it in the refrigerator overnight.

The next day, take the chicken out of the refrigerator. Peel one garlic clove and, using a mortar and pestle, a grater with small holes, or a knife, mash it into a purée. In a small bowl, stir together the garlic, Dijon mustard, about 2 tablespoons of olive oil, paprika, chopped thyme leaves, about ½ teaspoon salt, and black pepper. Stir together until a paste forms. Rub this paste all over the outside of the chicken. Stuff the cavity of the chicken with the unpeeled garlic cloves, quarters of lemon, and half of the thyme or savory branches. Let the chicken sit for at least 15 minutes.

While the chicken is resting, get a roasting pan ready. Add the carrots, turnips, potatoes, and about 1 tablespoon of olive oil. Salt lightly and toss everything together to coat evenly with the oil. Add the remaining branches of thyme or savory (or both). Place the chicken in the pan, breast side up, with the vegetables surrounding it, and cook for 20 minutes. Then remove the pan from the oven and turn the chicken over, putting the breast side down, and return it to the oven. After 20 minutes, turn the chicken back over and cook for 20 minutes more. If the chicken is on the large side, say 4 pounds or more, it will need an additional 15 minutes.

The way you can tell if the chicken is done is by looking at the drumsticks. If they are starting to pull away from the rest of the chicken, then it's ready. Another way to check is to make a small cut into the chicken with a knife and see if the juices that run out are clear.

Remove the chicken from the oven. Let it rest for 15 minutes so it cools down a little and the juices settle. This resting period will make the meat much more juicy.

To serve, cut the chicken into 12 pieces: cut the wings off the chicken, separate the legs from the thighs, and cut the thighs and breasts in half. Arrange the pieces of chicken on top of the roasted vegetables in the roasting pan or on a warmed platter, spoon the roasting juices over, and serve. (Everybody usually likes to get a piece of the breast!)

Tomatoes à la Provençale

Makes 4 servings

These tomatoes are delicious served hot or at room temperature, by themselves or with beans, lamb, or chicken.

> 6 to 8 tomatoes (about 3 pounds)
> ⅓ cup dry bread crumbs (page 97)
> 2 or 3 garlic cloves, minced
> 2 tablespoons parsley, chopped
> Sea salt
> Fresh-ground black pepper
> Olive oil

Preheat the oven to 450° F. Cut the tomatoes in half horizontally. Use a finger or the wrong end of a spoon to gently poke into each tomato half and loosen the seeds and juice inside. Turn each half upside down and gently shake out the seeds and juices into a small bowl. (If you want, you can strain out the seeds and drink the juice.)

In another small bowl, mix together the bread crumbs, garlic, and parsley. Salt lightly and add a few grinds of black pepper. Use a fork to gently mix it all together.

Lightly oil a glass or earthenware baking dish with olive oil. Arrange the tomato halves in the pan, cut-side up, so that they barely touch one another. Lightly season the tomato halves with salt. Spoon bread crumb mixture into each tomato half. Use your fingertips to tap the mixture into the tomato and keep adding more until the tomatoes are all filled. Drizzle olive oil evenly over the tomato halves. Bake in the oven for **30** minutes, or until the bread crumbs are toasty brown and the tomatoes are softened.

Beans Cooked over the Fire

*Makes about **6** cups*

I love cooking things over the fire—not only is it fun, but it makes things taste really good and smoky. We cook over a fire a lot, both outside on the grill and inside in our fireplace. If you don't have a fire handy, use a stove!

  2 cups dried beans
  1 small onion, peeled and cut in half
  5 or **6** garlic cloves, unpeeled
  1 bay leaf
  2 thyme sprigs

2 savory sprigs

Sea salt

Olive oil (optional)

Soak the beans overnight in at least **6** cups of water. They will swell and absorb lots of water, so make sure they're covered by **2** or more inches. (You don't have to refrigerate them while they soak.) The next day, drain the beans and put them in an ovenproof fire-safe ceramic pot. Add enough water so that it covers the beans by **2** inches. Add the onion, garlic, bay leaf, thyme, and savory—cooks call these "aromatics."

To cook the beans, you need the help of an adult. Build a small fire in a protected place—either in a fireplace or hearth or a barbecue or fire pit. In order to cook food over a fire, you need to let the fire burn for a while first so that it makes hot coals. This might take a half hour or so.

Once the fire has burned down to a bed of burning coals, have the adult place a grate or small stand over it, and put the pot of beans on top. Let the beans slowly come to a simmer and cook until tender, anywhere from **45** minutes to **1½** hours, depending on the fire. If you're using a stove, bring the beans to a simmer the same way.

After **45** minutes, begin tasting the beans for tenderness. You want them to be cooked all the way through so they are soft, but not cooked so much that they fall apart or are mushy.

When the beans are ready, season with salt, starting with **1** teaspoon and adding more if you need to. Let the beans rest for at least **15** minutes before serving. The beans taste really delicious with a drizzle of good olive oil.

Bouillabaisse (Provençal Fish Soup)

Makes 6 servings

This soup always makes me think of Lulu and Lucien. We make it together for big celebrations or special occasions or when friends catch some really good fish! It does take time to make and there are lots of ingredients, but you can totally do it if you make it in steps. You can do lots of it ahead of time, like making the fish broth, cooking the vegetables for the soup base, making the *rouille*, and toasting the bread. Then, when you are ready to eat, the final steps of warming up the soup and cooking the fish in it take just a few minutes.

For marinating the fish:

> 1½ pounds white-fleshed fish, such as halibut, rockfish, or lingcod
>
> 3 tablespoons olive oil
>
> 2 garlic cloves, sliced thin
>
> Saffron
>
> Fennel fronds (the feathery leaves) from 1 fennel bulb
>
> 6 parsley sprigs
>
> 6 thyme sprigs
>
> Zest of 1 lemon, peeled in long strips

For the fumet (fish broth):

> 1½ pounds halibut bones (or bones of another white-fleshed fish), rinsed well

1 leek

1 small onion

1 small carrot

2 garlic cloves, sliced thin

2 tomatoes, chopped

Bouquet garni of 1 bay leaf, 3 thyme sprigs, and 4 parsley sprigs

5 peppercorns

5 coriander seeds,

¼ teaspoon fennel seed

2 tablespoons champagne vinegar

8 cups cold water

Sea salt

For the rouille:

2 small red bell peppers

1 slice good country white bread, crusts removed

3 tablespoons *fumet*

Saffron

Cayenne pepper

1 ripe tomato, peeled and seeded

About 1 cup *aïoli* (pages 105–106)

For the soup:

¼ cup olive oil

1 small onion, diced

1 small fennel bulb, diced

1 leek, halved and sliced thin

1 carrot, diced

Saffron

2 garlic cloves, minced

Sea salt

3 fresh or canned tomatoes, peeled, seeded, and chopped

1½ pounds clams

Croûtons (page 96)

1 teaspoon champagne vinegar

¼ lemon

To marinate the fish:

Cut it in same-size pieces about 1½-inches thick. In a shallow dish, coat the fish pieces with the olive oil, garlic, a pinch of saffron, the fennel fronds, parsley, thyme, and lemon zest. Refrigerate for at least 1 hour.

To make the fumet:

Put the well-cleaned fish bones, leek, onion, carrot, garlic, and tomatoes into a stockpot. Add the *bouquet garni*, peppercorns, coriander, fennel seeds, champagne vinegar, cold water, and a good pinch of salt. Bring to a boil, then immediately lower the heat to a gentle simmer. With a spoon, skim off any foam that rises to the surface. Simmer for 40 minutes. Ladle the broth through a fine-mesh sieve to strain it. Please be careful, because the soup will be really hot!

Let the soup cool to room temperature. If you're making the soup for later in the day, cover the *fumet* and refrigerate it until ready to use.

To make the rouille:

Rouille is a spicy garlic mayonnaise. You use the *aïoli* recipe and then add roasted peppers to it to make it hot. Preheat the oven to **450°** F. Place the peppers on a sheet pan and roast them in the oven for **35** minutes, turning them with tongs every **5** to **10** minutes, until all sides are blackened and the peppers are soft but not falling apart. Remove the peppers from the oven and place them in a shallow bowl. Cover the bowl so that the peppers can steam as they cool. This makes it easier to peel off their skins. Once the peppers are cool, place each one on a cutting board and pull off its stem, trying to take as many seeds with the stem as you can. Use your fingers or a kitchen knife to peel off the charred skin and remove any other seeds.

Soak the slice of bread in the *fumet* with a pinch of saffron and a pinch of cayenne until the bread is very soft, about **10** minutes. Once it is soft, purée the bread and the liquid, the peppers, and the tomato in a blender until the mixture is smooth. Make the *aïoli* and then whisk in the pepper purée. Add salt and garlic to taste. *Voilà!*

To finish the soup:

Warm the olive oil in a heavy-bottomed soup pot over medium heat. Add the onion, fennel, leek, and carrot. Cook for **5** minutes, stirring a lot so that the vegetables do not start to burn or brown. Add a pinch of saffron and continue cooking and stirring for **3** to **5** more minutes, until the vegetables are soft. Add the garlic and a generous pinch of salt, and cook for **1** minute more. Add the tomatoes. Clean and scrub the clams and make the *croûtons.*

When you are ready to serve, add the *fumet* to the cooked vegetables in the soup pot and bring to a simmer. Add the champagne vinegar. Add salt to taste. Remember, the clams will put more salt in the soup when you add them, so don't salt too much!

Have a slotted spoon and bowl ready. Add the clams to the simmering soup and then cover. After **2** minutes, remove any clams that have opened with the slotted spoon and put them in a bowl so they do not overcook. As clams continue to open in the soup, keep removing them until all of them have opened and are cooling in the bowl. Throw away any unopened clams.

Add the fish to the simmering soup and lower the heat so it barely bubbles. After **3** minutes, check a piece of fish for doneness by splitting it open. If its flesh is whitish and not see-through at all, it is cooked. Once the fish is cooked through, put the clams back in the soup and taste the broth for seasoning. Add salt if you think it needs it, and the juice of the ¼ lemon.

Have **6** bowls ready and spoon equal amounts of fish, clams, and vegetables into each bowl. Ladle the broth over the seafood. Float the *croûtons* on top of the soup, spoon a little *rouille* over them, and serve.

Couscous Royal with Chermoula

Makes 6 servings

Couscous is great because it serves lots of people. And you can make lots of things to go with it, like vegetables or meat or both! A trick I learned is to use the chickpeas' cooking liquid, which is lightly flavored with cinnamon and onion, for the couscous. Just make sure to use enough water when cooking the chickpeas! *Chermoula* is a spicy North African herb sauce that gives dishes with vegetables or fish a real jump.

For the chickpeas:

1 cup (½ pound) dried chickpeas

1 small onion, peeled and quartered

½ cinnamon stick

1 small dried red chile

2 tablespoons olive oil

Sea salt

For the chermoula:

One 1-inch piece of fresh ginger, peeled and sliced

1 garlic clove

1 serrano chile, seeds and veins removed

½ cup olive oil

⅓ cup flat-leaf parsley leaves

½ cup cilantro leaves and stems

Salt

Juice of ½ lemon

For the braised vegetables:

1 small butternut squash (about 1½ pounds)

4 tablespoons olive oil

2 or 3 carrots (about ½ pound)

Sea salt

1 pound turnips or kohlrabi

1 teaspoon cumin seeds

1 teaspoon coriander seeds

Saffron

1 large onion, diced

One 14-ounce can whole tomatoes

½ teaspoon turmeric

Cayenne pepper

2 garlic cloves, finely chopped

1 teaspoon fresh ginger, finely grated

Salt

For the couscous:

2 cups water

2 cups organic couscous, regular semolina or whole wheat

2 tablespoons butter

1 teaspoon sea salt

To make the chickpeas:

Put the chickpeas in a bowl and add at least **4** cups of water, or enough to cover the chickpeas **2** or more inches above their level. Soak overnight. (You don't have to refrigerate them.) The next day, drain off the soaking liquid and put the chickpeas in a medium-size pot. Add enough water to cover the chickpeas by 1½ to 2 inches. Add the onion, cinnamon stick, chile, and olive oil. Bring to a boil, skimming off with a spoon any foam that floats to the top. Lower the heat to maintain a simmer and cook until the chickpeas are tender, anywhere from 45 minutes to over an hour. When the chickpeas start to soften, but before they are fully cooked, add a generous pinch of salt. Once they are cooked completely, remove the chickpeas from the heat and let them cool in their cooking liquid. Remove and discard the onion, cinnamon stick, and chile.

To make the chermoula:

Put the ginger, garlic, serrano chile, and olive oil in a blender or food processor and blend until smooth. Be careful with the chile, because if you get any on your fingers, anything you touch—like your face—can sting! Add the parsley and cilantro and blend until the leaves are chopped. Salt to taste. Then add the lemon juice. After you adjust the flavor the way you want it, set the *chermoula* aside until everything else is ready.

To cook the vegetables:

Preheat the oven to 400° F. Peel the squash, take the seeds out of the middle, and cut into 1-inch chunks. Put the squash chunks on a baking sheet, drizzle them with 1 tablespoon of the olive oil, and toss to coat them evenly. Season with a pinch of salt and spread in an even layer. Roast in the oven for 15 to 20 minutes, until tender. Set aside to cool.

While the squash is roasting, parboil the other vegetables. Bring a large pot of salted water to a boil. Peel the carrots and cut into 1-inch segments. Peel and trim the root vegetables and cut into 1- to 1½-inch pieces, either wedges or cubes. In separate batches, first cook the carrots and then the root vegetables in the boiling water until they are just tender, about **5** minutes. Remove the vegetables from the boiling water with a slotted spoon and spread on a baking sheet to cool.

In a small heavy pan over medium heat, toast the cumin seeds, coriander seeds, and a pinch of saffron just until they start to smell good. Then grind the spices to a powder using a mortar and pestle.

Heat a large skillet or heavy-bottomed pot over medium heat. Add the remaining **3** tablespoons of olive oil, the onion, and a large pinch of salt and cook for about **5** minutes, until the onion softens. While the onion is cooking, drain the tomatoes and cut into small pieces. Add the tomatoes to the skillet and cook for another **2** minutes. Add the toasted and ground spices, turmeric, a pinch of cayenne, garlic, and ginger and cook for **2** minutes more, stirring every now and then.

Add the chickpeas and their cooking liquid and bring to a simmer. Add the squash, carrots, and root vegetables. There should be a good amount of liquid from the chickpeas, but if you think it needs it, add **1** cup of water. It should be soupy. Taste for seasoning, adding more salt if necessary, and simmer for **5** minutes.

To make the couscous:

Bring **2** cups of water to a boil in a pot with a lid. Add the couscous, butter, and salt. Immediately cover and remove from heat. Let sit for **5** minutes and then uncover. Fluff with a fork, or your fingers, and then cover to keep warm until ready to serve.

To serve, put a scoop of couscous on each plate and then ladle the braised vegetables over it. Top it off with a spoonful of *chermoula*.

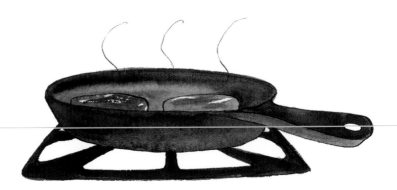

Steak Frites

Makes **2** *to* **3** *servings*

We only eat steak on special occasions, and when we do, my mom makes sure we get very special beef from the butcher. It comes from cows that are fed on grass their whole lives. We always share portions, because a little steak goes a long way—especially when you put the yummy compound butter on it and eat it with the crispy *pommes frites*! You can also pan-fry lamb chops or pork chops the same way.

> 2 rib eye or filet mignon steaks, 1½-inches thick
>   (5 to 7 ounces each)
> Olive oil
> Sea salt
> Fresh-ground black pepper

For the compound butter:

> 1 garlic clove
> 1 tablespoon thyme, chopped
> ¼ cup parsley, chopped
> 8 tablespoons unsalted butter, softened
> Lemon juice
> Sea salt
> Fresh-ground black pepper

An hour before cooking, take the steaks out of the refrigerator so they can warm up to room temperature. This helps the meat cook evenly.

Make the compound butter: pound the garlic to a paste. Then add the chopped thyme and parsley and the soft butter, mixing well. Squeeze some lemon juice on the butter and sprinkle with salt and pepper. Taste for seasoning, adjusting the salt and lemon if you think it needs it. Set aside until ready to use.

Right before cooking, put the steaks in a shallow pan or on a big plate. Drizzle with just enough olive oil to lightly coat both sides of the steaks. Season all the sides of both steaks generously with salt and pepper.

Heat a 9-inch cast-iron skillet or heavy-bottomed pan over medium-high heat for 5 minutes, until it is completely hot. Add the steaks to the pan, making sure that they are not touching. After 2 to 3 minutes, peek beneath a steak to make sure it is browning and not burning. Turn the heat down to medium and let it continue to cook for 4 minutes total. Flip the steaks over with tongs and cook on the other side for 4 more minutes.

Press the top of a steak with your finger. It will be soft if the steak is rare, a bit springy when it's medium rare, and firm when it is well done. If you're not sure, you can cut into the steak and peek at the meat inside. If you feel that the steak is still softer than you'd like, flip it over and cook for a few minutes more. Keep feeling it until it's just how you want it. (I find that a steak often takes **10** to **12** minutes to get to medium rare and medium, but my mom always tells me to check because each steak is different.)

Remove the steaks from the pan. Let them rest for **5** minutes to let the meat relax. Then carve and serve.

Pommes Frites (Crispy Pan-Fried Potatoes)
*Makes **2** to **3** servings*

You can fry the potatoes just before cooking the steak and then keep them warm in a preheated oven. Or, with the help of an adult, you can fry the potatoes at the same time that the steak is cooking. Russet Burbank potatoes are very starchy and make very crispy *pomme frites*, but all potato varieties are delicious.

> 1 pound medium-size russet potatoes
> Sea salt

¼ cup olive oil
Fresh-ground black pepper

Peel the potatoes. Cut them in half lengthwise and cut each half into wedges about ¾-inch thick. Boil the potatoes in a pot of generously salted water until they are tender when pierced with a fork, but not totally soft or falling apart. Drain and spread them out on a sheet pan to dry and cool. Line another sheet pan with absorbent paper or paper towels and set near the stove.

Heat a 9-inch cast-iron skillet over medium heat for a few minutes. When the pan is hot, add the olive oil. Carefully add enough potatoes to form a single layer in the pan. Let them fry without touching them, until they brown on one side. Depending on the kind of potato, this can take from 2 to 7 minutes.

Once the potatoes begin to brown, use tongs to turn each one over. Cook the potatoes on the other side until they are golden brown. Remove the finished potatoes with a slotted spoon and place on the towel-lined sheet pan. If you're not eating right away, keep the potatoes warm in a low oven, around 225°.

Just before serving, sprinkle the potatoes generously with salt and pepper. Serve them piled on a warm platter.

Fish en Papillote (Fish in Parchment Paper Packages)

Makes 4 servings

En papillote means "cooked in a paper parcel." It's kind of like cooking fish as a big present for everyone! In this version you don't make a real folded-up packet, but you cover the fish with a piece of parchment paper so that it steams as it bakes.

For the compound butter with fines herbes:

4 tablespoons unsalted butter, softened

¼ cup *fines herbes,* chopped (tender herbs like parsley, chervil, tarragon, and chives)

1 teaspoon shallot, finely diced

¼ teaspoon chopped or grated lemon zest

Sea salt

For the vegetables:

2 carrots, peeled

1 leek, white part only

½ fennel bulb, outer layer removed

For the fish:

4 fillets of sole or another white fish, such as rock cod (1 to 1½ pounds)

1 lemon, quartered

To make the compound butter:

Measure the butter, *fine herbes*, shallot, and lemon zest into a small bowl, and with a wooden spoon or fork, stir until completely combined. Add salt to taste.

To prepare the vegetables:

Slice the carrots into little matchsticks. You do this by trimming off one side of the carrot, setting it on its flat side, then slicing the carrot lengthwise into thin slices. Cut the slices into ⅛-inch-thick matchsticks.

Cut the leek in half lengthwise; if it is still too long, cut it in half crosswise, too. Slice into long, thin matchsticks.

Cut the fennel bulb in half, lay the flat sides on the cutting board, and cut the bulb into thin slices, from the root end to the stems. Lay these slices flat on the cutting board and cut them into matchsticks about the same size as the carrots and leeks.

Bring a small pot of well-salted water to a boil. Cook the carrots for 1 to 2 minutes, until they are just tender. Remove with a slotted spoon and let cool on a parchment-lined pan. Cook the leeks and fennel the same way, separately, just until tender, for 1 to 2 minutes. Spread out to cool on the parchment.

To make the fish:

Preheat the oven to 425° F. Pat the fish dry with a paper towel and season generously with salt. Prepare a roasting pan large enough to hold the fish fillets. If you are cooking sole, a larger roasting pan may be necessary, as the fillets are thinner and wider than those of other fish. Spread the blanched vegetables evenly on the bottom of the pan. Place the 4 fillets of fish on top of the vegetables, making sure to leave a little space between each one. Put a tablespoonful of compound butter on both ends of each fillet.

Cover the fish loosely with a large sheet of parchment paper. Bake for 7 to 10 minutes, checking for doneness after 7 minutes. When the fish is done, it will be opaque almost all the way through. Because the fish will continue to bake after it comes out of the oven, it is okay to take it out when it is slightly underdone. Sole will cook more quickly than other, thicker fish, so watch out!

Serve each portion of fish on a warm plate with the vegetables, a generous spoonful of the buttery juices, and a wedge of lemon.

Roasted Herbed Rack of Lamb

Makes 4 servings

When you go to the butcher, ask them to French cut a rack of lamb for you. They will know what you mean and trim it so that the ribs are cleaned off and the fat is removed.

1 rack of lamb, French cut

Sea salt

1 garlic clove

1 teaspoon thyme, chopped

1 teaspoon rosemary, chopped

1 tablespoon olive oil

About 1½ hours before cooking, remove the rack of lamb from the refrigerator. Put it on a plate and lightly sprinkle it all over with salt on both sides. Pound the garlic clove in a mortar and add the thyme, rosemary, and olive oil. Stir everything to mix it up. Rub this mixture all over the lamb and let it sit for 1 hour at room temperature.

Preheat the oven to 400° F. Set a cast-iron or other heavy-bottomed skillet over a medium-high flame. When the skillet is hot, sear the rack of lamb on both sides until each side is golden brown. When it is seared, put the pan with the lamb in it into the oven and roast for 10 to 15 minutes, until the temperature inside the lamb is 127° F. You can test with a meat thermometer. Just stick the thermometer into the center of the lamb and read the temperature.

When it's ready, remove the lamb from the oven and put it on a warm plate to rest for 5 minutes. Cut the lamb into chops and serve.

Potatoes au Gratin

Makes 6 to 8 servings

Something cooked *au gratin* is baked until it gets a brown crunchy crust. You can *gratiné* lots of things, but potatoes are my favorite. This goes great with the rack of lamb. If you can't find Yukon Gold potatoes, use another variety that has dense, waxy flesh, such as Yellow Finn or German Butterball potatoes. These kinds of potatoes are often called boiling potatoes. (Baking potatoes have crumblier, mealier flesh.)

3 tablespoons butter

2¼ cups heavy cream

¾ cup chicken broth (page 115)

1 bay leaf

German Butterball

Yukon Gold

Yellow Finn

Sea salt

4 pounds medium-size Yukon Gold potatoes

1 tablespoon thyme, chopped

Fresh-ground black pepper

Preheat the oven to 375° F. Smear about 1 tablespoon of softened butter all over the inside of a large earthenware, ceramic, or glass *gratin* dish, about 13 by 10 inches.

Measure the cream and chicken broth into a heavy-bottomed pot. Add the bay leaf and 1 tablespoon of salt and bring to a simmer, then lower the heat so that the liquid is only bubbling very gently. After 5 minutes, turn off the heat and let the bay leaf infuse its flavor into the cream.

Wash and peel the potatoes. Cut them into ¼-inch slices. To make cutting them easier, I slice the potatoes in half and place each half flat on the counter, cut-side down, before slicing them. You can also use a mandoline, if you have one, but if you do, make sure an adult is helping you and that you are using a safety guard!

Once all the potatoes are sliced, make layers of the slices in the buttered *gratin* dish, overlapping them a little bit like shingles on the roof of a house. When the first layer is done, sprinkle it with a quarter of the chopped thyme and some fresh-ground black pepper and salt. Keep making layers of potatoes, sprinkling each layer with thyme and salt, until no potatoes remain (usually about 3 to 4 layers).

Remove the bay leaf and slowly pour the cream mixture over the potato layers. The liquid should come up just below the top of the potatoes. To check, I press the potatoes gently with a spatula to see if the cream quickly rises over them. Dot the remaining 2 tablespoons of butter on top of the potatoes, then cover the *gratin* dish tightly with foil.

Bake covered for about 35 minutes, until the potatoes are almost tender when you poke them with a sharp knife. Remove the foil and turn up the oven temperature to 400° F. Press the top layer of potatoes down gently with a spatula to moisten them with the cream. Keep baking until the *gratin* is nicely browned, about 30 minutes more.

Remove from the oven and let rest for 10 minutes.

Variation

⚜ Sometimes we use vegetables like butternut squash, parsnips, or celery root in *gratins* too. They taste great and make the *gratin* kind of special. Alternate layers of potato with layers of the other vegetable and bake in the same way.

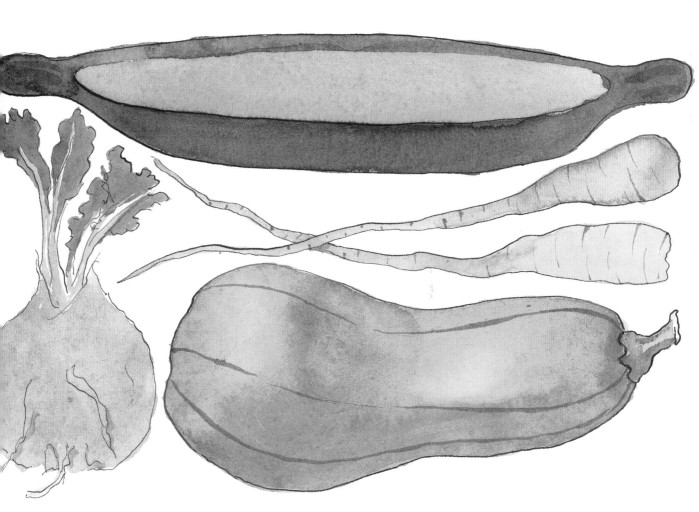

Les Salades

Lots of times you eat salad after the main course in France. I love salad so much, I eat it with every course! Or just have it for a course on its own!

Mesclun Salad

Makes **6** *servings*

Mesclun means "mixture" in the Provençal language (the language they used to speak in the South of France), and the best *mesclun* salad has a mix of lots of things: sweet young lettuces, spicy greens like rocket, whole leaves of herbs, and even edible flowers. Not all flowers are edible, so make sure someone helps you pick the right ones! This recipe makes a lot of salad, which is great if you're like me and love it!

6   generous handfuls (about ¾ pound) mixed lettuces, leaves, and herbs (Use tender young lettuces or the hearts of larger heads of lettuce, the yellow parts of curly endive, rocket leaves, mâche, young mustard leaves, parsley leaves, and chervil leaves.)

4   tablespoons *vinaigrette (page 105)*

Sea salt

Fresh-ground black pepper

A handful of edible flowers, such as chive blossoms, calendula petals, borage flowers, nasturtium, or pansies (optional)

To prepare the lettuces, separate the lettuce heads into leaves, getting rid of any damaged leaves you find along the way. Tear the larger leaves into smaller pieces but leave the smaller leaves whole. Wash all the lettuce gently in a large bowl filled with cold water. (If the lettuce is dirty, you may need to lift the lettuce out, change the water, and wash it again.) When the lettuce is completely clean, lift it out and spin it dry in a salad spinner. (Martine uses a dish towel: she puts the salad

in it and waves it over her head in her backyard!) If you use a salad spinner, only fill it half full; otherwise the leaves will be too crowded together and won't dry enough. It's really important to have dry lettuce, or the dressing won't coat the leaves when you put it on. As they are dried, spread the lettuce leaves out on a towel. Roll the towel up loosely.

When ready to serve, put the lettuce in a wide salad bowl. Pour half of the *vinaigrette* over the salad leaves and toss gently to coat, using your hands. The leaves should be lightly coated with dressing so they glisten. Taste the salad. If you need to, pour additional dressing over the salad and toss again. Add salt and pepper if needed. Sprinkle the salad with the petals of the edible flowers if you have them. Eat immediately.

Baked Goat Cheese with Garden Lettuces

Makes 4 servings

½ pound fresh goat cheese (one 2-by-5-inch log)
3 or 4 fresh thyme sprigs, chopped
1 small rosemary sprig, chopped
Toasted bread crumbs (page 97)

½ cup olive oil

½ pound garden lettuces, washed and dried

3 tablespoons *vinaigrette* (page 105)

Carefully cut the goat cheese log into **8** disks, each about ½-inch thick. (Hint: it's easiest to do this when the goat cheese is very, very cold.) Sprinkle the cheese disks with the chopped herbs and toasted bread crumbs and pour the olive oil over to marinate.

Preheat the oven to **400°** F. (A toaster oven works well too.) Carefully roll the cheese disks in the bread crumbs so they are evenly coated on all sides. Place the bread crumb–covered cheeses on a small baking sheet and bake for about **6** minutes, until the cheese is warmed completely.

In a large salad bowl, dress the lettuces with *vinaigrette*. With a metal spatula, carefully place **2** disks of the baked goat cheese on each plate. Put a small handful of salad next to the cheese and serve.

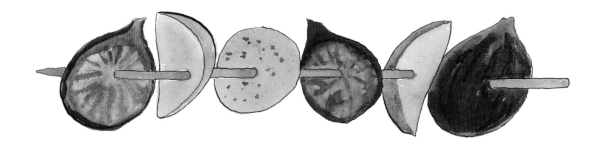

Les Desserts

Buckwheat Crêpes

*Makes **18** to **20** crêpes*

It's fun to make these and serve them to your friends right when they come out of the pan. You can pretend you have a *crêpe* cart just like the ones in the streets of Paris. You can serve *crêpes* plain or with fresh fruit like strawberries or jam. You can also stuff them with scrambled eggs or spinach. But then they're not really dessert!

¼ cup plain yogurt

¾ cup milk

⅓ cup water

2 eggs

3 tablespoons unsalted butter, melted

½ teaspoon vanilla

⅔ cup unbleached all-purpose flour

½ cup buckwheat flour

½ teaspoon sea salt

Sugar

Lemon juice

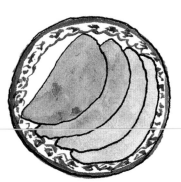

In a medium-size bowl, whisk together the yogurt, milk, and ⅓ cup water. Add the eggs one at a time, whisking until mixed. Whisk in the melted butter and the vanilla.

In another medium-size bowl, mix together the all-purpose flour, buckwheat flour, and salt. Make a well in the center of the flour mixture. Slowly pour the egg mixture into the well, whisking all the time from the center outward so you bring more and more of the flour into the liquid until everything is combined. When all of the flour is combined into the batter, whisk really hard for **1** minute. Let sit **15** minutes.

Heat an **8**- or **9**-inch *crêpe* pan or other heavy-bottomed pan over medium-high heat. Rub a small amount of butter on it and wipe away any extra with a paper towel. Ladle a thin layer of batter, about **3** tablespoons, into the center of the pan. Quickly tilt the pan in lots of different directions so that the batter spreads in a circle as thinly and evenly as possible. Cook the first side of the *crêpe* for **1** to **2** minutes until it's lightly browned on the edges. Loosen the edges with a butter knife or spatula and flip the *crêpe* over. Cook the other side for about **1** minute, or until that side is browned. Turn the pan over above a plate and let the *crêpe* fall out onto the plate. Rub the *crêpe* with a little more butter, sprinkle lightly with sugar, squeeze a little lemon juice over it, and fold it in quarters. Serve immediately.

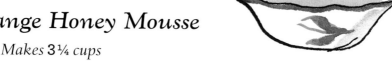

Orange Honey Mousse
Makes 3¼ cups

This mousse is somewhere between ice cream and whipped cream. It's really good on its own or with fresh, ripe fruit like figs, raspberries, or peaches. Make sure to get the best-tasting honey you can find. The better the honey, the better tasting the *mousse*!

1 tablespoon cold water
1 teaspoon gelatin
1 egg
¼ cup honey
¼ teaspoon grated orange zest

1⅓ cups whipping cream
1½ teaspoons orange juice

Measure the cold water into a small saucepan, sprinkle the gelatin over the water, and let it stand for a few minutes to soften.

In a small bowl, beat the egg with a handheld mixer at high speed for **1** to **2** minutes, until it thickens and becomes pale in color.

Heat the gelatin over very low heat, stirring constantly until it dissolves. Stir in the honey and continue to mix over low heat until the mixture is completely smooth. Add the orange zest and transfer to a bowl that will nest inside another, slightly larger bowl. Put just enough ice and water in the larger bowl that when you place the other bowl inside it, the ice water comes about halfway up the sides of the smaller bowl. Stir the gelatin mixture for a minute or two so that it cools and begins to thicken. Let it sit and continue cooling while you whip the cream.

In a separate bowl, whip the cream until it forms soft peaks. Whisk in the beaten egg and orange juice. Quickly whisk in the cooled honey mixture.

Cover and let chill for at least **2** hours. Serve a generous dollop with plates of ripe fruit such as figs, raspberries, strawberries, or peaches. If it is too thick, soften it by whisking lightly.

Chocolate Soufflé

Makes 6 to 8 servings

This *soufflé* recipe is great because you can make all the parts before dinner and then cook it really quickly right when you want to eat dessert.

Eight 4-ounce or six 5-ounce ramekins
2 teaspoons unsalted butter, melted
½ cup sugar
6 ounces dark chocolate (66% cacao)
¼ cup milk
1 teaspoon vanilla
1 tablespoon coffee
3 egg yolks
4 egg whites
Sea salt

Brush each ramekin generously with the melted butter, making sure to coat all of it—the bottom, sides, and lip. (This will keep the *soufflé* from sticking so that it will rise straight up.) Dust the ramekins with 2 tablespoons of the sugar, again making sure that each ramekin is thoroughly coated.

Chop 5 ounces of the chocolate coarsely (in rough pieces). Chop or grate the remaining 1 ounce very fine and set aside.

Make a double boiler. You do this by filling a medium-size pot with 2 inches of water and bringing the water to a simmer over low heat. In a medium-size bowl that you can set on top of the pot without having it touch the water, put the roughly chopped chocolate, milk, 2 tablespoons of the sugar, and the vanilla and coffee. Set the bowl on the pot and heat the ingredients in the bowl, gently whisking the chocolate until it is completely melted. Take the bowl off the pot and let it cool slightly. Add the egg yolks to the chocolate and whisk until completely blended.

In a clean stainless-steel bowl, using a whisk or handheld mixer, whip the egg whites until they become frothy. Add the remaining ¼ cup of sugar and a pinch of salt and whip until they form soft peaks. You'll know the egg whites are ready when you lift the whisk or beater out of the egg whites and a droopy peak forms. Gently fold the whites and the remaining 1 ounce of finely chopped or grated chocolate into the melted chocolate and egg yolk mixture.

Ladle the mousse into the ramekins, filling each ramekin nearly to the top. You can let the *soufflés* sit for up to 3 hours at room temperature before baking.

Preheat the oven to 400° F. When ready to bake, put the ramekins on a baking sheet and place the baking sheet in the oven for 8 minutes. The centers of the *soufflés* will remain soft and jiggly, but the outer edges will get cooked. Remove from the oven and let sit for 1 minute before serving. Be careful—the ramekins will be hot! I use a metal spatula to put each one on a pretty plate without touching them. The *soufflés* are great as is, but they can be topped with a dab of *crème Chantilly*. Yum!

Crème Chantilly

Makes about 2 cups

Whether you whip the cream by hand with a whisk or use a handheld mixer, make sure that the cream and bowl are both cold when you start. This will make it much easier and faster to whip.

- 1 cup cold heavy cream
- 1 tablespoon sugar, or to taste
- ½ teaspoon vanilla

In a cold stainless-steel bowl, whisk together the cream, sugar, and vanilla and keep whisking until the cream starts to get light and fluffy and forms soft, droopy peaks when you lift the whisk out of the cream. Don't whisk it too much or it will get too hard and grainy. Use immediately!

Fruit Kebab à la Troisgros

Makes 8 skewers

- 8 bamboo or wooden skewers
- 2 peaches or nectarines, ripe but still firm
- 2 plums or 4 apricots, ripe but still firm

4 to 6 figs

Juice of ½ small orange

1 teaspoon orange zest

2 tablespoons sugar

Soak the skewers in water.

Cut the peaches or nectarines in half and take out the pits. (If the pits are stubborn, use a little knife to gently carve around them.) Place cut-side down on a cutting board and cut each half into 4 large wedges, about 1 to 1½ inches thick. Repeat this process with the plums or apricots, cutting each half into quarters or halves, depending on how big they are. Cut each fig in half, taking care to trim off the toughest part of its stem.

In a small bowl, mix together the orange juice and zest. Take a skewer from the water and slide 4 to 5 pieces of fruit onto it, making sure to pierce through each chunk of fruit so that it stays on the skewer. Lay the fruit skewers flat in a shallow baking dish large enough to hold them all. Once all the fruit is skewered, sprinkle the orange juice and zest mixture over the skewers. Sprinkle the sugar evenly over all the pieces of fruit and let the skewers sit for 10 to 15 minutes before you cook them.

Preheat the broiler. When the oven is ready, brush the fruit once more with the orange juice in the baking dish and then place the skewers on a broiler-safe pan or aluminum foil. Broil the skewers for 8 to 10 minutes, or until the edges of the fruit are browning and beginning to give off juice. They should be cooked, but not falling apart.

Remove from the oven, let cool for a few minutes, and serve.

Martine's Tarte au Citron (Lemon Tart)

Makes one 11-inch tart (12 servings)

This tart has two parts: the *pâte sucrée* (crust) and the curd. If I can, I like to make the tart dough the day before and the lemon curd as well, if I have time. That way, when it's time to cook the tart, half the work has already been done.

For the pâte sucrée:

- 8 tablespoons unsalted butter (1 stick), at room temperature
- ⅓ cup sugar
- ¼ teaspoon salt
- ¼ teaspoon vanilla
- 1 egg yolk
- 1¼ cups unbleached all-purpose flour

For the lemon curd:

- 8 lemons
- 4 eggs
- 6 egg yolks
- 4 tablespoons milk
- ⅔ cup sugar
- ½ teaspoon salt
- 12 tablespoons unsalted butter (1½ sticks), cut into small pieces

To make the pâte sucrée:

Beat together the butter and sugar until creamy. Add the salt, vanilla, and egg yolk and mix until completely combined. Add the flour and mix

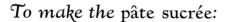

until there are no dry patches. Wrap the ball of dough in plastic wrap and press into a 4-inch disk. Chill several hours or overnight until firm.

Preheat the oven to 350° F. Remove the ball of dough from the refrigerator ten minutes before rolling it out. Cut two 14-inch-square pieces of parchment paper and sprinkle each one lightly with flour. Unwrap the dough and place it in the center of one of the floured parchments. Dust the top of the dough with flour and cover it with the other parchment paper. Roll out the dough between the papers into a 13-inch circle about ⅛ inch thick. If the dough sticks while you are rolling, peel back the parchment, dust again with flour, and replace the paper. I find it helps to flip over the parchment-wrapped disk midway through rolling. If excess flour remains after you are done rolling, peel back the paper and brush it off. Transfer the dough to a flat baking sheet and refrigerate for a few minutes to firm up.

To fill an 11-inch tart pan, remove the top sheet of parchment and flip the dough over, dropping the dough into the tart pan with the paperless side down. Peel off the remaining piece of parchment and then press the dough into all the corners and the fluted rim of the pan. Pinch off any excess dough hanging over the sides. If there are any cracks or gaps in the dough, press scraps into them to fill them in. Let the *pâte sucrée* rest in the freezer for 10 minutes before baking.

Transfer the *pâte sucrée* directly from the freezer to the preheated oven. Bake until slightly golden, about 15 minutes. Check the tart shell halfway through baking. If you see any bubbles making the dough rise, pat them down with a metal spatula. Remove the tart shell from the oven and let it cool before filling with the lemon curd.

To make the lemon curd:

Grate the zest of **2** of the lemons and set aside. Juice all the lemons, or as many as it takes to yield **1** cup of strained juice.

In a medium-size bowl, beat the eggs, egg yolks, milk, sugar, and salt until just mixed. Stir in the lemon juice and zest and add the pieces of butter. Transfer to a heavy nonreactive saucepan. (If they're used for acid ingredients like lemon juice, pots and pans made of aluminum, copper, or unseasoned cast iron become discolored and pitted and make food taste weirdly metallic. Stainless steel, enameled cast iron, glass, ceramic, and well-seasoned cast-iron are all nonreactive—but if you choose glass or ceramic, make sure it's safe to use the pan over a burner.) Heat over medium heat for several minutes, stirring constantly with a spatula or wooden spoon, until the mixture becomes thick enough to coat the spoon. Be careful not to let it boil or the eggs will curdle. When the mixture has thickened, turn off the heat. Place a strainer over a stainless-steel, ceramic, or glass bowl and pour the warm lemon curd through the strainer to remove any lumps. Cover with plastic wrap. If not using within **1** hour, refrigerate until ready to use.

To assemble and bake the tart:

Preheat the oven to **375°** F. Make sure the prebaked tart shell has cooled, then fill it with the lemon curd. Smooth out the lemon curd with a spatula and bake until the lemon curd is set, **15** to **20** minutes. Serve warm or at room temperature, with *crème Chantilly* (page **162**), if you like.

Almond Brown Butter Cake

Makes 10 to 12 servings

This cake is really good, and it's not super sweet. I've had it for dinner and lunch and sometimes even for breakfast.

- 1½ cup sliced almonds
- 12 tablespoons unsalted butter (1½ sticks)
- 1 teaspoon lemon juice
- 1 cup plus 2 tablespoons sugar
- ½ cup flour
- ½ teaspoon salt
- 4 eggs
- ½ teaspoon vanilla
- ¼ teaspoon almond extract

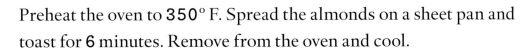

Preheat the oven to 350° F. Spread the almonds on a sheet pan and toast for 6 minutes. Remove from the oven and cool.

Melt the butter in a small saucepan. Brush some of the melted butter onto the bottom and sides of a 9-inch cake pan. Continue to cook the rest of the butter over medium-low heat for 10 to 20 minutes, until it becomes golden brown. Remove from the heat and stop the butter from cooking by adding the lemon juice. Set aside to cool.

Spread ½ cup of the sliced almonds evenly on the bottom of the cake pan. Dust the almonds in the cake pan with 2 tablespoons of sugar.

Grind the remaining 1 cup of almonds in a food processor until the almond pieces are the size of little grains. In a medium bowl, mix the ground almonds with the flour and salt.

Crack the eggs into a large mixing bowl and add the remaining **1** cup of sugar. Using a whisk or an electric mixer, beat the eggs fast for about **5** minutes, until they thicken, increase almost **3** times in volume, and turn a pale yellow.

Gently sprinkle half the ground almond mixture over the beaten eggs. With a spatula, gently fold the almonds into the eggs. When the ground almond is halfway folded in, add the rest and continue to fold gently until everything is evenly mixed. Carefully fold in the brown butter and vanilla and almond extracts. Pour the batter into the cake pan over the sliced almonds and bake on the center rack of the oven for **35** to **40** minutes. You'll know the cake is done if you poke a wooden skewer or toothpick into the middle and it comes out clean.

Remove the cake from the oven and let it cool on a rack. When completely cool, run a knife around the edges of the cake to separate it from the pan. Put a flat plate over the top of the cake pan and then flip them both over quickly, so that the cake pan is now on top of the plate. Remove the pan, banging on its bottom if the cake sticks at all.

Serve as is or with a little *crème Chantilly* (page **162**).

Tisanes (Herbal Infusions)

Makes 2 servings

Lemon Verbena

You can make great hot herbal drinks by pouring hot water over really fresh and good-smelling herbs and spices. The water releases the herbs' flavors and starts to taste like them. This is called "steeping" the herbs. Lots of times my mom and I have a lemon verbena *tisane* after we have lunch or dinner. Other times we make one out of mint. You can use lots of different kinds of herbs to make *tisanes*, and other plants make good infusions too, such as ginger or a stalk of lemongrass. If my stomach's upset, I make a ginger *tisane*, and lots of times it helps me feel better. When I have a cold, my mom makes a *tisane* out of lemon thyme and I put my head under a towel with it and inhale its vapors (just like I showed Brigitte!). Even rose petals make good *tisane* (if you're sure they haven't been sprayed with pesticides)! Try your own combinations and experiment—I like orange peel with rosemary (and maybe a little honey)—and you'll find the things you like best and figure out how long you should steep them for.

> **A big handful of herbs**
> **2 cups boiling water**
> **Honey (optional)**

Place the herbs in a pitcher or teapot and pour the water over them. Let steep for a few minutes and then pour the infusion into little cups or glasses and serve.

Les Confitures

Good jams catch the taste of ripe fruit right at its very peak. This way you can taste good fruit all year long!

Plum Jam

Makes about 3½ cups

1½ pounds Santa Rosa plums

2 cups sugar

1 teaspoon lemon juice

Wash the plums and cut them in half, twisting the halves slightly to separate them. Remove the pits, either with your fingers or with a small knife. Cut each plum half into thin wedges, about ¼- to ⅓-inch thick. Place all the plum wedges in a heavy stainless-steel pan, along with the sugar and lemon juice. Stir to mix it all together and let it sit for **30** to **60** minutes (or overnight in the refrigerator). The sugar will dissolve and the plum juices will release.

Put a little plate in the freezer. To cook the jam, bring the plums and sugar to a boil over medium heat, stirring every minute or so. As the jam boils, a little foam will form on the top. Use a spoon to skim this off. (I like to have a little bowl nearby where I can put all of the foam.) Keep boiling the plums gently for about **10** minutes, stirring with a wooden spoon or rubber spatula every now and then. After **10** minutes, as the liquid evaporates, start stirring more often to make sure that no jam starts to stick to the bottom of the pan.

After about **5** more minutes, or when the jam gets thicker, remove the plate from the freezer and put a small spoonful of hot jam on the plate. It will cool right away, and if you like its thickness—thick enough so it doesn't run on the plate when you tilt it—then the jam is ready. If the jam is still very runny, then keep cooking for a few minutes more and test again on the chilled plate.

When the jam is done, put it in a bowl or in jars or on some toast! You can keep it in the refrigerator until you eat it all up!

Variation

✢ Plum-raspberry jam: add **1** pint of raspberries to the plums at the beginning and let them all sit in the same amount of sugar before cooking.

Roasted Strawberry Jam

*Makes about **2** cups*

3 pints strawberries, hulled and quartered (about 5 cups)
3 cups sugar
1 teaspoon lemon juice (optional)

Mix the strawberries and sugar together in a bowl. Taste the strawberries and see how sweet they are. If they are really sweet, add the lemon juice. If they are just right, leave them alone. Let the sugar-covered strawberries sit for at least **30** minutes at room temperature, or you can put them in the refrigerator overnight.

Preheat the oven to **350**° F. Spoon the strawberries into a **9**-by-**13**-inch glass dish and cover with aluminum foil. Bake for **30** minutes. Take off the foil, lower the temperature in the oven to **250**° F, and keep baking for **3** more hours, stirring the strawberries every **45** minutes or so. After **3** hours, the jam will still look like it has too much liquid, but that's okay. Turn off the heat and let the jam sit overnight in the warm oven. By morning, the extra juice will have evaporated and the jam will be thick and the strawberries will look like they are hanging in their thick red juices.

Spoon the jam into clean jars, cover, and refrigerate. The jam will keep for up to **6** weeks.

Translation of French Words and Phrases

À droite!: To the right!

À gauche!: To the left!

À table!: To the table!

Ah . . . la vie: Ah, life.

Ah! Très belle, n'est-ce pas?: Ah! Very beautiful, isn't it?

Alors: So.

Apéritifs: Drinks served before a meal as an appetizer.

Au revoir!: Good-bye!

Avez-vous passé un bon été?: Did you all have a good summer?

Baguette: A long skinny loaf of French bread.

Bassin: Bay.

Bien sûr: Of course.

Bienvenue, les enfants!: Welcome, children!

Boeuf bourguignon: A beef stew originally from Burgundy.

Bon appétit: Enjoy your meal ("good appetite").

Bouillabaisse: A hearty fish soup.

Ça va?: How are you doing?

C'est Manon et Fanny!: It's Manon and Fanny!

C'est pas possible!: It's not possible!

Citrons pressés: Lemonades.

Comme la politique!: It's like politics!

Cornichons: Little pickles.

Domaine: An estate.

Est-ce que je peux goûter les carottes?: May I taste the carrots?

Excusez-moi, madame, c'est une jolie fleur. Où l'avez-vouz achetée?: Excuse me, madame, that is a pretty flower. Where did you buy it?

Fantastique!: Fantastic!

Fêtes: Parties.

Fraises des bois: Wild strawberries ("strawberries of the woods").

Fromage frais: A creamy, soft fresh cheese.

Galette: A round flat pastry.

Gratin: A baked dish with a browned crust of bread crumbs or cheese.

l'Huître: Oyster.

Huîtres sauvages: Wild oysters.

Incroyable!: Amazing!

J'ai une idée!: I have an idea!

Ma petite chérie: My little dear.

Macaron: A kind of Parisian cookie.

Macédoine: A salad of cut-up fruit or vegetables.

Magnifique!: Magnificent!

Mais oui!: That's right! But of course!

Mer: The sea.

Merci!: Thank you!

Mise en place: Ingredients prepared, organized, and ready to go ("putting in place").

Moi!: Me!

Moi aussi!: Me too!

Un Moment!: One moment!

Mon dieu!: My god!

Oeufs farçis: Stuffed eggs.

Oui: Yes.

Ouvrez vos cahiers et prenez vos crayons!: Open your notebooks and take out your pencils!

Pain au levain: A French country-style sourdough bread.

le Pain est la culture!: Bread is culture!

Pan bagnat: A Provençal sandwich of tuna and vegetables.

Parfait!: Perfect!

Pas de problème!: No problem!

Pétanque: A French outdoor bowling game.

le Poisson: Fish.

Regarde, Fanny, très spécial, non?: Look, Fanny, very special, don't you think?

Regardez!: Look!

Rillettes: A pâté-like dish of meat cooked in fat and shredded.

Rouille: A garlicky sauce with roasted peppers.

Sabayon: A light egg yolk dessert.

Salade niçoise: A salad named after the city of Nice.

Salut!: Cheers!

Santé!: Your health!

Sauce verte: Green sauce.

Saucissons: Cured sausages resembling salami.

S'il vous plaît, asseyez-vous!: Please take your seats!

S'il vous plaît, madame, est-ce que je peux avoir un biscuit?: Please, Madame, may I have a cracker?

Socca: Chickpea flour pancake.

Soufflés: Baked airy desserts made with egg whites (literally, "blown").

Soupe au pistou: A vegetable soup made with vegetables and topped with *pistou* (a basil sauce).

Tant pis!: Oh well!

Tapenade: A spread made with chopped olives, garlic, and olive oil.

Tisane: A refreshing tea made by soaking fresh herbs in hot water for a short time.

Tout ce qu'il faut!: Everything that's needed!

Tout le monde: Everybody.

Très cher!: Very expensive!

Très facile: Very simple.

Très sauvages: Very wild.

Tuile à l'orange: A delicate orange cookie.

Vendangeur: A person who harvests grapes in the vineyards.

La Villa les Clairs Matins: The Villa of the Clear Mornings.

Vinaigrette: A salad dressing made with oil and vinegar.

Vive la France!: Long live France!

Voilà!: There it is!

Vous êtes les filles de Pagnol!: You are the daughters of Pagnol!

Almonds
with Sage

Beans Cooked
over the Fire

Oeuf Mayonnaise

Mesclun Salad

François's
Marinated Olives

Crudités

Mayonnaise

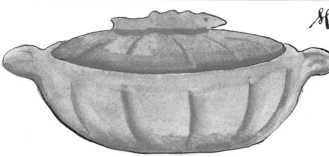

Bouillabaisse

Mesclun

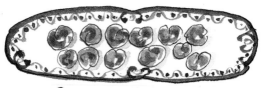

Gougères

Croûtons